Our Eyes Fixed
On Jesus

Our Eyes Fixed On Jesus

A Sideways Look at Spiritual Warfare

Guy Chevreau

New Wine Press

New Wine Ministries
PO Box 17
Chichester
West Sussex
United Kingdom
PO19 2AW

ISBN 1–903725–75–5

Typeset by CRB Associates, Reepham, Norfolk
Cover design by CCD, www.ccdgroup.co.uk
Printed in the United States of America

"Our good Lord,
with all the tender love He has for all those that shall be saved,
comforts readily and sweetly . . . .
It is true that sin is the cause of all this pain,
But all shall be well,
And all shall be well,
And all manner of all things shall be well."

(Julian of Norwich, *Revelation of Love*, AD 1373)

Contents

Endorsements

"I devoured Dr. Guy Chevreau's latest book. In *Our Eyes Fixed On Jesus*, he challenges some of the myths and extreme views on spiritual warfare that exist today in the Body of Christ. This book will empower readers to live free from superstition and fear, and experience the true knowledge of Jesus Christ and the power of His Holy Spirit."

Dr. David E. Carr
Senior Minister, Renewal Christian Centre, Solihull, England
Regional Overseer, Free Methodist Church, UK

"I grew up in an era amid a setting that had a list of forbidden words. At the top of the list and of equal negativity were the words 'tongues' and 'demons'. When the Holy Spirit brought a reviving to the church where I pastored, the forbidden words became common fare. We entered into the world of spiritual warfare and hand-to-hand combat with real demons with real people experiencing real deliverance. Soon we found ourselves overwhelmed by the number of people wanting and needing help. Our staff was consumed with spiritual warfare and deliverance and having a great deal of success. Soon, a balance of emphasis and practice became an absolute necessity.

This book is a welcome declaration on the positive – yes, even joyous – side of spiritual warfare. The bad news is we are at war. The good news is Jesus has already won it. In this splendid work, Guy lays a solid foundation for both the required tension and balance that makes for a joyous journey in waging the war. Enjoy the adventure of worship amid conflict!"

Jack Taylor
President, Dimensions Ministries
Melbourne, Florida

"It is a privilege to recommend this latest book by Guy Chevreau who has been a dear friend for the past ten years. The Church emerging from the wilderness of obscurity throughout the world is marked by a dynamic confrontation with demonic powers. Guy Chevreau tackles the subject of spiritual warfare to lead us to a biblical understanding. In this book he shows us how to fix our eyes on Jesus, fill our minds with Christ, and thus be empowered for effective spiritual warfare in everyday life."

Charlie Cleverly
Rector of St Aldates Church, Oxford

Foreword

From Rolland:

As Christians we know we have an adversary, the devil, who prowls around like a roaring lion seeking someone to devour. He has deceived and destroyed many lives. The question is, exactly how should we wage war against the prince of this world and all his demon hordes?

The subject of spiritual warfare commands much attention these days and in some circles it is a major focus of entire ministries dedicated to intercession and winning battles in the land against forces of darkness. Much has been experienced and written, but questions, problems and controversy continue to arise.

This book by our close friend Dr. Guy Chevreau is a tremendous resource, adding balance and completeness to our understanding of spiritual warfare. His detailed research and illustrations make a powerful case for concentrating more on Jesus than on the devil, empowering us to take authority over demonic power as we follow the Holy Spirit's lead.

Guy's careful study of Scripture demonstrates a gloriously positive side to spiritual warfare, one that emphasizes the beauty and glory of our Saviour Jesus and the all-sufficiency of the Gospel. Our power and authority lies in our intimacy with Him, and we fast and pray in order to worship and enjoy Him more deeply, and to experience even more hunger for Him. In other words, we engage in spiritual warfare not just to be rid of negative influences, but to be filled up to overflowing with the Kingdom's righteousness, peace and joy in the Holy Spirit!

Negative confrontation cannot by itself motivate and sustain us; we need to be ravished by His presence in order to be victorious against the enemy.

From Heidi:

We now live in Mozambique, Africa, where the general population commonly experiences the supernatural realm. We heard testimony in church this week from a woman who had been very ill with acute asthma for ten years. Because of some of her involvements, she was as demonized as anyone that has come to our church in Pemba. She was healed of asthma and set free instantly by prayer and a hug filled with the love of Jesus. Her husband was amazed by her healing and the transformation of her life, although he continued to drink and fly into crazy rages. One day he had a demonic fit and died. After he was pronounced dead at the hospital his wife began to pray in Jesus' name. In a little over an hour he was raised from the dead – and came straight to the church to ask Jesus into his heart! He was set free from the demons who had tormented him for years and this morning at church he announced with a huge smile that he has not had a drink of alcohol since that day.

In my early years as a preacher, I would spend countless hours praying for the demonized to be set free. I would ask the demons their names, yell, fight and cast them out, often long into the night. Most of those I prayed for were set free, but I was left exhausted! Guy's book shows another way: authority through intimacy with God and the power of love. The closer we are to our all-powerful King, the easier deliverance is. *We will always win through love.*

After reading Guy's book, I had a personal victory over one of the last remaining fears in my life. I have a bad history with wild dogs. As a runner I have often been chased by snarling dogs. One day on a prayer walk on a beach in Mozambique, for instance, a pack of wild dogs surrounded me and forced me into a salt-water river filled with sharks. I screamed at the dogs, rebuking them in Jesus' name. I bound the devils in the local language, Shangaan, then in English, Portuguese and tongues! I fought furiously, but was terrified that they would rip me to shreds. Eventually they turned on each other and started ripping into each other's flesh. I was safe, but shaken and exhausted.

When I finished reading *Our Eyes Fixed On Jesus*, I went for a prayer walk accompanied by my collie and two Labs. Suddenly a pack of dogs descended from a hill at full speed, barking, growling and baring their teeth. I calmly began to sing, *There is no fear in the perfect love of God*. The love of Jesus took away all fear from my heart. I was filled with the peace of Jesus and confident of my deliverance. The dogs fussed over us for a while and then left as quickly as they had appeared. This time I was free, but without stress and exhaustion. Thank God for His victory over the powers of darkness, and for Guy's book.

Heidi and Rolland Baker
Pemba, Mozambique
May 2006

Acknowledgements

Thanks go to Nev Green – you were the first one to hear most of these musings. Your questions and reflections helped shape this work in so many ways.

Thanks also to Susanna Celso, Anne Fountain, Lois Francis, Eddie and Sue Mason and Dr. Dave Mullen. Your careful reading of the manuscript, and your comments and corrections have made *Eyes Fixed On Jesus* a better book.

Peter and Chris Drown, and Tom and Karen Henner – thank you for your support and encouragement, especially down the final stretch. You helped keep my head clear.

Lastly, to my wife Janis – thank you for all your help on so many fronts. As first reader, your critique is invaluable. Yours is a big part in this book.

Guy Chevreau
Oakville, Canada
April, 2006
S.D.G.

Introduction

"Never aim at what you don't want to hit."
(Lee Trevino, professional golfer)

Spiritual warfare is not a subject that I find immediately engaging and this was not a book that I particularly wanted to write. It began as a sermon series, that at the request of two of my regular church hosts. As I prepared for the conferences, and subsequently extended the research and reflections, however, my understanding has slowly turned.

My time in study and prayer have brought me to a place where I believe that the message is more about worship than it is warfare. Over sixteen-hundred years ago one of the church fathers, John Chrysostom, felt similarly. He prefaced his sermon series *On the Power of Demons* by saying: "We [preach] this, not because our discourse about the devil is sweet to us, but because the doctrine about him is full of security for you." [1]

The second time through my sermon series, a woman approached and thanked me for the teaching. She was beaming, so I asked, "How has the Lord met you over the course of our weekend together?" She proceeded to tell me that she worked for a ministry located in Little Five Points, in downtown Atlanta. It is a haven for runaway kids, drugs and prostitution, and she described it as one of *the* demonic strongholds in the region, possibly even the state. It is certainly a very creepy

---

[1] John Chrysostom, *Three Homilies Concerning the Power of Demons*, II.1, Nicene and Post-Nicene Fathers, First Series, vol. 9, Hendrickson Pub., Peabody, Mass., 1994, p. 187.

place. The storefront for a shop called the Vortex is a two-story skull. Some of the Little Five Points' clientele "dress" themselves extravagantly at the Ink Wizard tattoo parlour, while others frequent the Voodoo clothing store. There is also a shop promising to meet "all your occult needs".

This woman felt called to be a light for Christ in the darkness, but was ever aware that she was continuously "under attack". She told me that as she fed the homeless and offered prayer to those who would receive it, a witch would regularly come out of her store and harass and curse her. It had previously been profoundly disturbing and so unsettling that the woman had wondered if she could or should continue to try to bring the Gospel into such hostile territory.

She then said, "After this weekend, I can't wait to get back!" I asked why. In her gentle Southern drawl the woman answered, "Next time that witch starts cursing me up one side and down the other, I now know that I can look her straight in the eye and say, 'Sugar, I'm not the one at risk.' "

The name we gave to the sermon series was "Our eyes fixed on Jesus – a sideways look at spiritual warfare." Nev Green, pastor of the Gathering Place in Blandford Forum, Dorset, was the ministry host who initially asked for teaching on the subject of warfare. He did so because there were those in the church family who were spreading some seriously "wonky" ideas around. The title of the conference, and this book, was chosen to convey the approach and the purpose of the teaching from the outset.

The first phrase, "Our eyes fixed on Jesus", is taken from the opening verses of Hebrews 12:

> *"With this great cloud of witnesses around us, therefore, we too must throw off every encumbrance and the sin that all too readily restricts us, and run with resolution the race which lies ahead of us, our eyes fixed on Jesus, the pioneer and perfecter of faith."*

The "cloud of witnesses" refers to the great Old Testament heroes of faith, Abel, Enoch, Noah, Abraham and Sarah, Isaac, Joseph, and Moses, as well as the unnumbered heroes and heroines who *"overthrew kingdoms, established justice* [and] *saw God's promises fulfilled".*[2] Though the term spiritual warfare is not used in the passage, it is clear that these witnesses were very much "under attack" – some were tortured to death; others flogged, fettered and imprisoned. *"They were stoned to death . . . sawn in two . . . put to the sword . . . deprived, oppressed, ill-treated."*[3] In the midst of all, the exercise of their faith was to keep their *"eyes fixed on Jesus".*

The second phrase of the title, "a sideways look at spiritual warfare", is a recognition that we should give only peripheral consideration to Satan and spiritual warfare. The prince of darkness and his works must never have our front and centre attention. As men and women of faith, it is never ours to show more concern, interest or effort fighting the devil than worshipping and serving our risen Lord. Eight hundred years ago, Teresa of Avila put the issue succinctly: "I do not understand these fears which make us cry, 'Oh, the devil, the devil' when we might be saying 'Oh God, oh God!' and making the devil tremble."[4]

Two different prayers follow. As you read them, attend to the feelings and impressions that they evoke.

The first:

> *"In the name of Jesus Christ I take authority over any and all spirits of the kingdom of darkness that would come against the writing, publishing, distribution and reading of this book, against me or my family, against its readers and their families. I forbid all spirits of darkness from having any access to this*

2 Hebrews 11:33.
3 Hebrews 11:35–37.
4 *The Life of Saint Teresa*, trans. J.M. Cohen, Edinburgh, Penguin Books, 1957, p. 183.

book or interfering in any way. I bind you with chains that cannot be broken.

Together, as author and reader, we confess any sins that would give any rights or grounds to the enemy and we pray that the light of Christ would shine on any dark angels sent to confuse or disrupt the reading of this book. In the name of Jesus, we cancel every assignment of the enemy and we come against every demonic influence. We command that every familiar spirit leave our spheres and never return.

I cancel any curse, hex or spell sent against me and all those reading this book, from anywhere in the kingdom of darkness, and send them back to their source.

All this I do in the name and authority of the Lord Jesus Christ. Amen."

The second:

"Jesus, we rest in the fullness of Your precious name – 'Saviour'.

Draw our hearts ever deeper in Your love and be our Way, our Truth and our very Life.

Thank You that You hold all things together – our all.

You are the Christ, 'The Anointed One'. As we open our lives to You, we ask that You come to us, and bring release to that which is still captive, and sight to all that is still blind. Bind up what's broken and grant us Your favour.

Holy Spirit, as I write this book and as others read it, confer upon us ever-more wisdom and understanding, that the eyes of our hearts may be enlightened, that we may know the hope to which You call us, how rich and glorious is our inheritance, and how vast the resources of power open to us who have faith. Reveal to us more of the Kingdom righteousness, peace and joy that is purposed for us.

Lord, our hearts cry out – 'Your Kingdom come' – in us, through us, and by us.

Thank You Jesus, that You have rescued us from the domain

of darkness, and brought us into Your Kingdom. Thank You that our release is secured and our sins are forgiven.

You are the light of the world and You give the light of life. Everything exposed to light becomes light; send forth Your light and Your truth to be our guide; draw us into Your dwelling place – there, we lay everything before You, for You and You alone are our joy and delight.

Father, we humble ourselves before You, that we might know more of Your grace and we pray that out of the treasures of Your glory, You would grant us strength and power in our innermost being, that Christ may dwell in our hearts in love. Lord, let it yet be ever-more established deep within us – the length and breadth, the height and depth of Your love for us in Christ; may we know it, knowing that this love is ever-beyond our understanding. Lord, fill us with this knowledge, that we would be filled with Your very fullness. Father, may we live with the expectation that You are ever doing immeasurably more than all we can ask or even conceive, all to Your glory, now and forever more.

Thank You, Father, that You purpose to conform us to the very image of the Lord Jesus; renew our minds, that our whole nature be thus transformed.

Holy Spirit, fill us with peace and joy, until we overflow with hope and make us whole and holy, through and through, spirit, soul and body, free of any fault. Amen."

The first prayer is focused primarily on the enemy and his works, and has little by way of explicit biblical grounding. The phrase, "the kingdom of darkness", for instance, does not appear anywhere in Scripture. The apostle Paul asserts that Christ has *"rescued us from the domain* [exousia] *of darkness and brought us into the kingdom of his dear Son, through whom our release is secured and our sins are forgiven"*.[5] Spiritual darkness is only a power. It is not and cannot be a kingdom, for only a

---

[5] Colossians 1:13.

prince rules over it. In Christ, we have been rescued by the King and brought into His Kingdom.

The second prayer is composed entirely of Scripture and is directed to the Trinity.[6] A number of biblical prayers make up the core and as the great reformer John Calvin wrote 350 years ago, one does not err when one "reposes on the Word and promise of God", for it is the "sole end and legitimate use of prayer, that we may reap the fruits of God's promises".[7] The second prayer is also longer than the first and un-apologetically so. Its extended length is a reminder that the Lord's desire to bless is so much greater than the evil one's to curse.

In researching this work, I have drawn from the insights of some of the earliest theologians, the church fathers. Their understanding of the demonic and warfare predates the con-structs of our generation by at least 1,500 years. They are, therefore, so much closer to sharing the mindset, worldview and understanding of Jesus and the early Church. Furthermore, the early Church was preoccupied with Christ and very much alive to the presence and the power of the Holy Spirit dynamically at work in their midst. They were a "committedly missioned" people who knew that they lived as citizens of another world, *"aliens in a foreign land"*[8] as the apostle Peter called them. They were not pandering after Rome's values and the Empire's decadent lifestyle; theirs were Kingdom values and Kingdom priorities.

They were also a fearless people. Justin Martyr (apologies for the pun, but his name is a dead giveaway) testified before the Romans, his executioners, "Since our thoughts are not fixed on

---

[6] The phrase-by-phrase Scripture references can be found in Appendix A.

[7] *Calvin's Commentaries*, vols. IV, Psalm 7:6, p. 81 and VI, Psalm 119, p. 428, Baker Book House, Grand Rapids, 1993.

[8] 1 Peter 2:11.

the present, we are not concerned when men cut us off. Death is a debt which must at all events be paid."[9]

Persecution has a unique way of keeping the faith and theology pure, passionate and focused.

This book is more an exposition of Christology than demonology and more about our position and authority in Christ than the nature and strategies of the demonic hosts that rage against us.

It is my hope and prayer that it serves to bring you, my brothers and sisters, to a place of glorious freedom and confident authority, in the knowledge that though we live in the midst of a very real conflict, we're not the ones at risk.

---

[9] *Ante-Nicene Fathers*, vol. 1, Henderickson Pub., Peabody, Mass., p. 166.

Chapter 1

Fear and Freedom

"Fear and darkness were now on every side;
but not on those who had seen the light
of God's countenance."
(John Wesley, 19th September 1745)[1]

My doctor prescribed Lariam as the anti-malarial medication for my first trip to Mozambique. The information sheet that accompanied the drug assured me that "the benefit of this medication is greater than the risk of its side effects". Some of the listed contra-indications included, "hair loss, vomiting, diarrhoea, numbness in the hands and feet, depression, psychotic episodes and suicidal ideation". These I successfully dodged. What I did suffer were "strange dreams", the inter-active kind. One night, I was viciously attacked by a huge black dog. Attempting to protect myself, I lashed out and kicked him as hard as I could. Regrettably, my wife Janis was left with a size 11 bruise on her thigh the next day.

In all sorts of ways, every one of us has suffered unintentional woundings from our loved ones. Unfortunately, it gets worse: in Zechariah 13:6 the prophet asks the question: *"What are these scars . . . ?"* The answer he receives names a disturbing reality: *"I got them in the house of my friends."* We could all bear our scars and tell our sorry tales of betrayal by those closest to us.

---

[1] *The Journals of John Wesley*, London, Thomas Tegg and Son, 1836, p. 221.

Worse still, we suffer a very real attack from a very real and malicious enemy. Sadly, it's not just that unfortunate circumstances undeservedly befall good people.

It was nearly twenty years ago that I first accepted the fact that we actually had a foe that actively warred against us. Frank Peretti's novel, *This Present Darkness*, opened up a whole new world. When I read it, I kept thinking of my own experiences as the young rookie pastor of Rockland Drive United Baptist Church in the small rural town of McAdam, New Brunswick. Just like Pastor Hank Busche, the protagonist in the book, I too was confused, discouraged and frustrated because I wasn't seeing the fruit I expected of my ministry. Page after page of Peretti's book vividly described an invisible realm of angelic and demonic spirits in open combat, at war over the souls of the saints. The malicious work of principalities and powers was graphically detailed and it was uncertain whether the "good guys" would prevail.

The book left me feeling uncomfortably vulnerable. If honest, I felt a measure of fear I'd never known before. Demonic spirits suddenly seemed to be everywhere, at work in nearly everything.

Peretti's book and its sequel, *Piercing the Darkness*, have sold over three and a half million copies. They have been formative influences for countless readers, and while they may be engaging fiction, unfortunately, they are very misleading theology.

The most repeated imperative in all of Scripture is: *"Do not be afraid."* It recurs over three hundred times and is never an empty admonition. Its first occurrence sounds the reason for the call to fearlessness. In the early chapters of Genesis, Abram leaves the comforts and securities of home and family in answer to God's call on his life, but he soon finds himself in hostile territory. After his first victory the high priest Melchizedek names the source of Abram's triumph: *"Blessed be God Most High ... who has delivered your enemies into your hand."* [2] Later that night, God comes to Abram in a vision and adds further revelation saying, *"Do not be afraid ... I am your shield."* [3]

The Lord is not only a God who both protects and fights for His beloved; in Genesis 26:24 His nature and disposition are further revealed. In this passage, the Lord appears in the night to Isaac, who was wearied by his ongoing conflict with the Philistines, and says to him: *"I am the God of your father Abraham ... I am with you, so do not be afraid. I shall bless you...."*

In Greek, the word for fear is *phobos*, the etymological source of "phobia". Its root means "to flee, to run". Arachnophobia is the fear of spiders. I have a missionary friend who is irrationally afraid of what he calls "evil spiders".

At one level it is appropriate to speak of the gift of fear; emergency fear is the release of adrenalin and dopamine, the body's rocket fuel. Under its influence the heart suddenly pumps five gallons of blood a minute instead of one and the blood vessels constrict to reroute blood flow from the skin and organs to the brain and muscles. The liver dumps glucose into the bloodstream to produce a further surge of energy and the nostrils flare to facilitate an increased oxygen intake. The pupils dilate for maximum visual perception. Endorphins are released from the neo-cortex to increase the pain threshold and we are then ready for "fight or flight". Depending on the size of the evil spider, my missionary friend either beats it to a pulp or sprints away and has a little shudder.

On the other hand, long-term, anxious fear doesn't empower. Rather, it has the opposite effect: it debilitates, even paralyses. It is also very profitable: 2.5 billion dollars are spent on anti-anxiety drugs annually.

Fearlessness, however, is the Lord's preferred prescription, for though there are forces at work that pose very real threats to

---

2 Genesis 14:20.
3 Genesis 15:1.

our wellbeing, He would have us know that in Him we have
the resources to overcome.

The psalmist knows this truth. He writes, *"I lie down and
sleep;* [by implication, eight hours later] *I wake again, because the
LORD sustains me. I will not fear the tens of thousands drawn up
against me on every side."*[4] Forget facing *tens of thousands* – most
of us toss and turn all night if we're afraid that our boss is mad
at us. What then, is the source of biblical fearlessness? In the
best-known Psalm of all, the answer is unquestionably clear:
relationship. *Though I walk through the valley of the shadow of
death, I will fear no evil, for you are with me."*[5]

In the book of Isaiah, providential care is further promised:

> *"This is the word of the LORD, the word of your Creator . . .
> Have no fear, for I have redeemed you; I call you by name;
> you are mine. When you pass through water I shall be
> with you; when you pass through rivers they will not
> overwhelm you; walk through fire, and you will not be scorched
> . . . I am the LORD your God, the Holy One of Israel, your
> deliverer."*[6]

In Christ, this experience of relational immediacy deepens.
Jesus says, *"I am the light of the world. No follower of mine shall
walk in darkness; he shall have the light of life."*[7] The context
for this declaration, while not explicitly one of warfare, is
certainly conflictual. Jesus subsequently makes a categorical
assertion: *"You will know the truth, and the truth will set you
free."*[8]

When teaching on this, I produce a twenty-dollar bill, wave it
about and say, "Anyone here who'd like this?" Hands go up all

[4] Psalm 3:5–6, NIV.
[5] Psalm 23:4, NIV.
[6] Isaiah 43:1–3.
[7] John 8:12.
[8] John 8:32.

around the sanctuary. "What if I could demonstrate that it's a counterfeit? The ink's not right. There are no watermarks in the paper and the texture's all wrong. Any interest? How many know that if you tried to spend it, you could end up in a lot of trouble?" In a small measure, the truth sets, or at least, keeps us free.

When one understands the truth about pornography – that all it can offer is counterfeit intimacy – there is a significant release from its hold. Similarly understood, the psychic has nothing but counterfeit prophetic revelation. (Why is it we never read the headline, "Psychic wins lottery again"?)

Fear can also be counterfeited. We were made to fear: *"The fear of the LORD is life; he who is full of it will rest untouched by evil."*[9] We are invited to *"taste and see that the LORD is good. Happy are they who find refuge in him! Fear the LORD, you his holy people; those who fear him lack for nothing."*[10] Healthy, holy fear is an aspect of worship and right relationship with God and issues in blessing and prosperity. *"Happy are all who fear the LORD, who conform to His ways. You will enjoy the fruit of your labours, you will be happy and prosperous."*[11] Distorted, counterfeit fear, in contrast, makes us afraid. When the psalmist was *"panic-stricken"* at the torments of his enemy, his heart *"torn with anguish"*, the *"terrors of death"* crushing down upon him he says: *"fear and trembling have beset me; horror has overwhelmed me."*[12] Worry, anxiety and torment are the counterfeits of awe, reverence and wonder.

When we're afraid, we don't just forfeit our peace and wellbeing; we ultimately give the devil the attention he seeks. Our "afraidness" is the corrupt, distorted worship he craves. Things can thus be contrasted: Psalm 100 exhorts us to *"Enter [God's] presence ... with thanksgiving and His courts with*

9 Proverbs 19:23.
10 Psalm 34:8–9.
11 Psalm 128:1.
12 Psalm 55:3–5, NIV.

praise."[13] When we get all wound up and throw our little tantrums, we've come into the devil's "presence" and entered his realm with our anxious fears.

A glorious freedom and authority is established when we know the truth about fear. In a warfare Psalm, we read this testimony:

> *"The LORD is my light and my salvation –*
> *whom shall I fear?*
> *The LORD is the stronghold of my life –*
> *of whom shall I be afraid? . . .*
> *Though an army besiege me,*
> *my heart will not fear;*
> *though war break out against me,*
> *even then will I be confident."*[14]

The case can be made that the psalmist wasn't just under attack from hostile human enemies, for he writes: *"When evildoers close in on me to devour me, it is my adversaries who stumble and fall."* Cannibalism was not a military practice in the ancient Near East. Fear can, however, be so consuming that it seems to devour at least one's confidence and peace.

It also enslaves, so that outside of the grace of God, we live a *"life of fear"*.[15] But the apostle Paul asserts that as the adopted children of God, we have a new Spirit, one which enables us to cry *"Abba! Father!"* In the intimate knowledge of His unfailing love there is not only peace, freedom and security; as heirs of God and fellow-heirs with Christ, authority, boldness and invincibility are also ours. With Paul, each of us ought to be able to declare:

> *"I am convinced that there is nothing in death or life, in the*
> *realm of spirits or superhuman powers, in the world as it is or*

---

[13]   Psalm 100:2, 4.
[14]   Psalm 27:1, 3, NIV.
[15]   Romans 8:14.

*the world as it shall be, in the forces of the universe, in heights
or depths – nothing in all creation that can separate us from the
love of God in Christ Jesus our Lord.*"[16]

When we are unconvinced of this glorious truth, the best we
can do is try to survive. As we don't have sufficient resources in
and of ourselves, however, there is a dismal sag and whimper to
the living of our lives. Or worse. There are those who suffer
from all manner of distorted phobias: if once scared by the
attack of a big dog, that fear is twisted so that one is now afraid
of all dogs, even little yappers.

As real as these terrors seem to be, there are deeper, more
pervasive fears, the things that keep us awake at two o'clock in
morning. The fear of insufficient finances. The fear of an
uncertain future. The fear of sickness – if not for ourselves, then
for our children's health and safety. The fear of premature death,
or death itself. The fear of others' judgments, criticisms and fault-
finding. The fear of demonic attack. The fear of a Satanist's curse.

In contrast, the beloved disciple boldly writes, *"There is no
fear in love. But perfect love casts out fear, because fear has to do with
punishment."*[17] As the preceding verse speaks of *"confidence
on the day of judgment"*, most English Bibles translate *kolasin*
as "punishment", but the word could equally be rendered
"torment", as the KJV and NKJV do. Luther translated the phrase,
"fear has its own agony". Certainly experience confirms that
when we're suffering a panic attack it feels more like torment
than punishment.

Relief comes by way of deliverance; fear is "cast out" – the
very language used in the Gospels as those demonized are set
free from their torment. John is repeatedly insistent that it is a
revelation of love that expels the torment. In many ways,
the issue is not so much getting the fear out, as it is getting the
love in.

[16] Romans 8:38–39.
[17] 1 John 4:18, NIV.

My dear friend Nev Green has learned this truth well. Two years ago, he spent a week teaching in the Iris Bible school in Bangula, southern Malawi. One afternoon, his host, a Canadian missionary, Mo, took him to visit a pastor who had been absent from the school for a few days following the death of his baby daughter. The pastor lived in a remote village in the bush. After a rather arduous journey, Mo and a couple of Malawian pastors went to see the village pastor and Nev took out his guitar and began to worship. It wasn't long before the white man with his guitar, singing next to a Swiss Army Pinzgauer, the ultimate 4×4 off-road vehicle, drew quite a crowd from the village.

Shortly thereafter, Mo and the other pastors returned and the preaching began. The message was simple and immediate: the God who made the mountains and forests that surrounded them was also the One who loved and cared for them. To demonstrate this love, they invited those who were sick to come forward for prayer. Most of those who responded were suffering from the various symptoms of malaria. All who were prayed for said that they had been healed of the presenting symptoms – the blinding headaches, fever, chills and acute nausea.

As Nev worked his way along the prayer line he came to an older woman who was kneeling next to a teenage boy. The woman asked him to pray for her son, Francis. The boy appeared to be severely mentally disabled. His mouth was open, drool ran down his chin and his eyes were unfocused. The boy's mother explained that as a young child Francis had suffered from cerebral malaria and it had left him mentally disabled and violently epileptic. His habitually violent fits happened nearly every night and were so violent that they frightened both his family and their neighbours.

Mo had joined Nev and together they began praying. As they waited on the Lord, Nev noticed a cotton bracelet on the mother's wrist. He asked if it was a witch-doctor's charm. She said that it was not. They continued to pray.

Francis' father arrived and Nev asked again whether they had taken Francis to a witch-doctor, emphasising that it was important that they knew the truth in order to pray for Francis in the right way. Eventually the parents showed them a charm around Francis' neck, hidden under his shirt. They were evidently frightened. Francis' father said that since the witch-doctor had given him the charm the fits had not been so violent. The father was convinced that if the charm was removed, the violent fits would begin again. He was insistent that only the witch-doctor had the power to take off the charm.

Nev and Mo debated with the parents while an increasing number of villagers looked on. Nev took a stand: "The charm cannot heal your son, but Jesus can." He asked them to choose which "remedy" they wished to believe in. The father reluctantly allowed him to remove the charm from Francis' neck. Nev then asked the parents to get Francis to kneel in front of him and hold his head so that the two of them were eyeball to eyeball.

Nev declared the victory of Christ over the works of the destroyer and spoke freedom from all that was cursed in Francis' life, blessing him in the name of Jesus. He continued to speak blessing over him, proclaiming that the Kingdom of Heaven was upon him and repeatedly spoke the love of Christ over him and into him.

As he prayed, Francis' eyes suddenly came into focus and, for the first time, he was looking at Nev and not through him. A smile gradually began to appear on his face and for the first time they'd been together, he spoke. His first words? "Jesus loves me."

Francis' father leapt about with joy and Francis began laughing. He seemed to be completely normal with no sign of any mental disability whatsoever.

A few days later the village's pastor returned to the Bible school. He was thrilled to report that Francis had not had a single epileptic fit since the afternoon's ministry and that the boy remained in good health.

Chapter 2
Who's On Our Side?

"Know the enemy, know yourself;
your victory will never be endangered."
(Sun Tzu, *The Art of War*, c. 4 BC)[1]

✣ ✣ ✣

Life in the Spirit is like riding a bicycle – balance is everything. One can fall off on either side. This is certainly the case with spiritual warfare. Sixty-five years ago, C.S. Lewis put it this way in his magnificent work, *The Screwtape Letters*:

> "There are two equal and opposite errors into which our race can fall about the devils. One is to disbelieve in their existence. The other is to believe, and to feel an excessive and unhealthy interest in them."[2]

For most of my Christian life, I fell off on the left. While at seminary we received no instruction on deliverance. Instead, we majored on counselling. One "came to terms" with one's torment. People weren't demonized, they were just really messed up. This demythologized mindset affected our interpretation of Scripture. Legion, for instance, wasn't really demonized. In a post-Freudian world he was simply a psychotic suffering schizoid paranoia, a psychotherapist's job security.

---

[1] Sun Tzu, *The Art of War*, ed. Samuel Griffith, Oxford, 1963, p. 129.
[2] C.S. Lewis, *The Screwtape Letters*, Fount Paperbacks, Glasgow, 1941, p. 9.

It wasn't until 1992 that I went to my first conference on deliverance. New to these things, I seated myself at the back, as near to the door as I could get, just in case. After some rather suspect teaching, we went into what was called a "ministry time". I'd never heard of such a thing. Within minutes a very large gentleman three rows ahead of me stood to his feet and began screaming at the top of his lungs. He then proceeded to throw the folding chairs around him. It was time for this good Baptist to exit, post haste.

Though that conference was less than a good experience, I subsequently found myself thrown into the deep end without my water wings. Pastorally, I was confronted with both overt demonic manifestations and the realities of "principalities and powers" that were very much set against my attempts to preach the Gospel. In the process, I read voraciously and made initial attempts at binding and loosing, rebuking and casting out. In retrospect, it seemed more like mud wrestling than deliverance and we certainly took a fair bit of beating in the process.

I wish I knew then what I know now. As I look back on those years, I realize that things had become pretty goofy. In my new-found zeal it seemed that nearly everything was warfare. If I tossed and turned at night I would rebuke tormenting spirits. No consideration was given to the six pieces of meat lovers' pizza I'd devoured just before retiring. Things got wilder. If we ran out of gas on the way to a conference, "the devil didn't want us to get there." I've since come to realize that if you don't pay attention to the fuel gauge, you're not under attack, you're under-intelligent.

Balance requires continuous attentiveness. As I have travelled to over 225 different churches over the last twelve years, an observation has been confirmed again and again: where there is a heavy emphasis on warfare, a spirit of fear is evident in the ways a congregation conducts itself. It always exacts a high toll, for fear is a thief. It steals our peace, our hope, our joy and our confidence.

With a view to heeding C.S. Lewis' counsel, the following is an attempt at establishing some foundational teaching on the demonic, while not nurturing an excessive or unhealthy interest in the darkness. There is a long and established precedent for this approach.

In AD 230, one of the church fathers, Origen, wrote a treatise titled *On the Principles*. His chapter, "On the Opposing Powers" stands as one of the earliest theological considerations of spiritual warfare. In introducing his considerations, Origen says of the devil, demons, and their opposing influences:

> "What they are or how they exist is not explained [in Scripture] with sufficient clarity. It seems that the devil was an angel; and having apostasized, he persuaded as many angels as possible to fall away with himself; and these are now called demons."[3]

If one will forgive the pun, Origen is saying that the origins of the demonic horde are veiled in mystery. As revealed in Scripture, the devil and his works receive nothing but peripheral consideration. The reason? We are to fix our attention on Jesus.

Cosmology is the technical term given to the study of beginnings. The opening verses of Genesis give poetic voice to creation's origins: *"In the beginning God created the heavens and the earth. The earth was a vast waste, darkness covered the deep . . . ."* Other translations describe the earth as "formless and empty" or even "a wreck and a ruin". At face value, it is puzzling that God should create a chaotic, desolate, wasted earth. Why wasn't it created perfectly, an Eden everywhere?

In Job 38:4–11 there is a veiled reference to the beginnings of

---

[3]   *Ante-Nicene Fathers*, vol. 4, Hendrickson Pub., Peabody, Mass., 1994, p. 240.

evil. Out of the whirlwind, God asks Job a series of questions He knows that Job cannot answer: *"Where were you when I laid the earth's foundations? ... Who fixed its dimensions? ... Who stretched a measuring line over it? ... On what do its supporting pillars rest? Who set its corner-stone in place, while the morning stars sang in chorus and the sons of God all shouted for joy?"* Though the point of this exchange is to bring Job to a place where he humbles himself before the sovereign majesty of the Almighty, the questions imply initial perfection in creating the earth. There is also a passing reference in verse 7 to the *"sons of God"*, or *"angels"* as the NIV translates. While no details are given, they seem to be some created beings, subordinate to God, in existence before the creation of the heavens and the earth.[4]

It is of further note that in Isaiah 45:18, *"the Creator of the heavens ... who made the earth and fashioned it ... created it not as a formless waste"*. The RSV translates the verse, *"He did not create it a chaos"*. In this, the Hebrew of Genesis 1:2 is both ambiguous and problematic, and a study Bible should have a note with an alternate rendering, as the NIV does: *"Now the earth* **became** *formless and empty... "* (emphasis added).

All of this has led many interpreters to posit what Oswald Chambers names "a great hiatus" between the first and second verses of the opening chapter of Genesis. Things need to be put on "pause" after citing the opening words: *"In the beginning God created the heavens and earth"*, for there followed a "celestial catastrophe" before the calling forth of the rest of creation.[5] Chambers (along with many others) quotes the pre-existent *"sons of God"* passage cited in Job 38 above and then brings

---

[4] KJV, NKJV, RSV, NASB, NEB, NET and JB all translate the literal Hebrew, "sons of Elohim/God". Other references include Job 1:6; 2:1; Pss. 29:1; 89:7.

[5] *The Complete Works of Oswald Chambers*, Discovery House Publications, Grand Rapids, 2000, p. 137. One of the earliest to interpret along these lines is John Cassian, c. AD 420, in *Conferences*, NPNF, Second Series, vol. 11, pp. 377–379. See also M. Lloyd-Jones, *Christian Warfare*, The Banner of Truth Trust, Edinburgh, 1976, p. 71; Michael Green, *I Believe in Satan's Downfall*, Hodder and Stoughton, London, 1981, pp. 36–41.

Ezekiel 28:12–17 to bear. It is a lament raised over the *"King of Tyre"*.

"This is what the Lord GOD *says: you set the seal on perfection; you were full of wisdom and flawless in beauty. In an Eden, a garden of God . . . you were on God's holy mountain . . . blameless in your ways . . . until iniquity came to light in you . . . Your beauty made you arrogant; you debased your wisdom to enhance your splendour. I flung you to the ground."*

Because there were no kings before the first man, Adam, the King of Tyre is no human, earthly king, but a superior, heavenly being, presumably one of the Job 38:7 *"sons of God"*. Further, Eden is not as it is described in Genesis 2. In Ezekiel's vision, Eden is full of precious stones; there are no trees in this garden, nor is there mention of the serpent, and there is no woman.[6]

There is, nevertheless, a fall in this Eden. Pride, arrogance and a quest for self-glorification drove this celestial being to attempt to usurp the place he was assigned by God.

Another passage, Isaiah 14:11–17, is used to trace further the origins of evil. It is again a prophetic picture, this time of the rebellious King of Babylon, also a heavenly being:

"Your pride has been brought down to Sheol, to the throng of your victims . . . . Bright morning star, how you have fallen from heaven, thrown to earth . . . . You thought to yourself, 'I shall scale the heavens to set my throne high above the mighty stars; I shall take my seat on the mountain where the gods assemble . . . . I shall ascend beyond the towering clouds and make myself like the Most High!' Instead you are brought down to Sheol, into the depths of the abyss."

---

[6] John L. McKenzie, "Mythical Allusions in Ezekiel 28:12–18, *Journal of Biblical Literature*, vol. 75, 1956, p. 326.

One other passage of Scripture receives consideration. In the twelfth chapter of the Revelation, the apostle sees a vision that takes him back in time – a third of the stars are swept from the sky and are thrown to earth. These are the angels that had joined in the cosmic rebellion and were hurled to the earth along with the bright morning star.[7] These fallen angels now constitute the demon horde.[8]

In summary then, there is some evidence to indicate that before the creation of humankind an unsuccessful mutiny took place. For those unsure of naval technicalities, a mutiny is defined as a "revolt against constituted authority on the part of subordinates". The balance of created order was then brought into being after this first fall, in the midst of a cosmic rebellion, under the rule of the one Jesus calls *"the prince of this world"*.[9]

With all of this in hand we can now continue reading Genesis 1:2: *"The earth was* [or *became*] *a vast waste, darkness covered the deep. . . . "* The celestial catastrophe is the cause of the desolation, waste and darkness that mars God's good creation.

No conjecture is required for what then follows: *"God said, 'Let there be light,'* . . . *and God saw that the light was good, and he separated light from darkness."* Under God's sovereign authority, unbounded darkness is limited to night. Darkness is diminished and restrained, and given a beginning and an end.

The balance of the Scriptures, from Genesis 1:2 through to Revelation 22:21, is the account of God's restoration and re-creation of the chaos caused by the pre-cosmic fall. Humankind is to play an active part in this redeeming work: in Eden, Adam and Eve are given the charge to *"be fruitful and increase, fill the earth and subdue it"*.[10] They are to extend the borders

---

[7] Revelation 12:4–9.

[8] John Cassian, *Nicene and Post-Nicene Fathers*, Second Series, vol. 11, p. 378. See also M. Lloyd-Jones, *Christian Warfare*, The Banner of Truth Trust, Edinburgh, 1976, p. 72.

[9] John 12:31; 14:30; 16:11. See Kallistos Ware, *The Orthodox Way*, Mowbray, Oxford, 1979, p. 74.

[10] Genesis 1:28.

of Eden's perfect order, bringing further restoration and redemption to that which is still chaotic and waste.

Four hundred and thirty years ago, John Milton wrote a long meditation on creation, *Paradise Lost*. In describing Satan's fall, Milton alludes to Ezekiel 28, Isaiah 14 and Jude 6. Once cast out, Satan declares: "To reign is worth ambition, though in hell; better to reign in hell than serve in heaven." [11] As succinct and insightful as those words are, pride was not the only reason for Lucifer's fall. Psalm 8:3–6 in the NKJV reads,

> *"When I consider Your heavens, the work of Your fingers . . .*
> *What is man that You are mindful of him,*
> *And the son of man that you visit him?*
> *For You have made him a little lower than the angels,*
> *And You have crowned him with glory and honour.*
> *You have made him to have dominion over the works of Your*
> *   hands;*
> *You put all things under his feet."* [12]

An unnamed rabbi wrote a treatise titled *The Life of Adam and Eve*, probably a century before the birth of Christ. It reads as a commentary on Ezekiel 28, Isaiah 14, Genesis 3 and Psalm 8:3–6, for in it the devil accosts Adam, saying, "It is for your sake that I have been hurled from that place [Heaven]. When you were formed, I was hurled out of the presence of God and banished from the company of the angels." What follows is an explanation: the Lord presented Adam to the assembled heavenly host and the archangel Michael calls them all to pay homage to the one made in the image of God.

---

[11] John Milton, *Paradise Lost*, Odyssey Press, Indianapolis, 1976, Bk.1.263, p. 13.

[12] Following the Septuagint, Syriac, Targum translations and Jewish traditions, the KJV and NKJV translate the phrase in verse 5, "lower than the angels". NIV translates the phrase "lower than the heavenly beings".

Lucifer's proud and mutinous spirit is revealed in his response: "I will not pay homage to someone who is lower than I am and who comes after me. I am his senior in the Creation and it is his duty to pay homage to me."[13] The angels under Lucifer follow his rebellious lead and also refuse to pay homage to Adam. God consequentially banishes them all from their position of glory and hurls them to the earth.

Only something like this scenario makes sense of the cryptic reference in Jude 6:

> *"Remember too those angels who were not content to maintain the dominion assigned to them, but abandoned their proper dwelling-place; God is holding them, bound in darkness with everlasting chains, for judgment on the great day."*

And if there is only a measure of truth in this interpretation of Lucifer's fall, the words of Jesus take on even greater significance as they sound dramatic counterpoint:

> *"The Son of Man did not come to be served but to serve, and to give his life as a ransom for many."*[14]

Whether or not one accepts the double fall theory – first the angels, then man – this much is uncontested: the origins of evil are shrouded in mystery. While beginnings are only hinted at, the evil one's malevolent mission is given much clearer description. In the seventh chapter of the Book of Daniel. The prophet has a dream which, given its subject matter, could well be considered a revelatory nightmare. He sees four beasts: a lion with wings like an eagle, a bear that insatiably gorges itself on flesh, a leopard with four wings and

---

[13] *Pseudepigrapha of the Old Testament*, ed. R.H. Charles, vol. II, Oxford University Press, 1913, p. 137.

[14] Matthew 20:28.

the last beast, *"exceedingly fearsome and exceedingly strong"*, with great iron teeth and bronze claws. His name and nature: the *Devourer*.

> *"He will hurl defiance at the Most High and will wear down [literally "wring out"] the holy ones of the Most High ... for a time, and times, and half a time. But when the court sits, he will be deprived of his sovereignty ... and greatness of all the kingdoms under heaven will be given to the holy people of the Most High."* [15]

This is no human despot, but a spiritual being, maliciously set against the purposes and the people of God; one seeking his own glory, jealously defiant of the place that the holy ones have in the heart of God. He seeks to instil fear and despair in the saints, *"for a time, and times and half a time"* [16] While the origins of the Devourer are not disclosed, his nature and authority are clearly defined. The enemy of the Lord's people is a contingently free being, exercising a limited authority, for a limited time, under the absolute sovereignty of God. The Devourer was *"waging war on the holy ones and proving too strong for them until the Ancient in Years came. Then judgment was pronounced in favour of the holy ones of the Most High ... "* [17]

There is one other scene from Daniel's dream that must be recounted. It is a most graphic foretelling of the end that is to come. Daniel sees:

> *"One like a human being coming with the clouds of heaven; he approached the Ancient in Years and was presented to Him.*

[15] Daniel 7:7, 19, 25–27.

[16] I was meditating on that last phrase and reflecting on the long and very hard season my wife and I had been enduring, when it seemed that I suddenly had an answer to my heart's cry, "How long, Oh Lord?" – "Three and a half times longer than you figure it should last." I am slowly beginning to recognize that my timelines are considerably shorter than the Lord's.

[17] Daniel 7:21–22.

Sovereignty and glory and kingly power were given to him, so that all peoples and nations of every language should serve him; his sovereignty was to be an everlasting sovereignty which was not to pass away, and his kingly power was never to be destroyed.''[18]

All prophetic visions require interpretation. Some may choose to understand the passages from Ezekiel 28, Isaiah 14 and Daniel 7 differently and draw other conclusions. There is, however, clear and incontestable revelation conveyed in the names Scripture assigns to Satan, especially when contrasted with the names given to Jesus. The comparison graphically details their respective missions and mandates.

The name "Satan" in Hebrew means "adversary"; "Jesus" means "Saviour". The devil is called our "enemy"; Jesus is known as "the friend of sinners". The name "Lucifer" means "bright morning star"; but the morning star is outshone when the "Light of the world" rises to shine on those who live in darkness. The "dragon" is defeated by the victorious "Lamb". "Belial" – "the worthless one" – is a pathetic contrast to the One to whom all the saints cry, "Worthy!"

The "murderer's" work is undone by the One who is not only "the Giver of Life", but "the resurrection". The "father of lies" is impotent before the "Truth". The "thief's" mission is ever thwarted by "the Giver of every good and perfect gift" and the "deceiver" is no match for the "Revealer". The "prince of this world" has no authority over the "King of kings", for the "prince of the power of the air" must submit to the One who is "above all government, authority, all power and dominion". The "Son of God" came to destroy the works of the "destroyer"; the "Deliverer" to save us from "the tempter". One is either a child of the "heavenly Father" or the "evil one", choosing to live under the authority of either the "Alpha and

[18] Daniel 7:13–14.

Omega, who was, and is, and is to come", or "the god of this passing age", either the "God of the living" or "Beelzebub" the "lord of the flies" – literally, "the dung god". One worships either "the Christ, the Anointed One", or "the anti-Christ, the un-anointed one".[19]

I read philosophy for my BA and that caused me a few problems at seminary. When we got to Matthew 4 in the New Testament survey course, I put up my hand and asked, "Doesn't the temptation in the wilderness evidence a metaphysical dualism that is antithetical to radical Judaic monotheism?" I wasn't trying to show off; I just wanted to know, because it seemed to me that the account put Jesus and the devil on a level playing field. My question was not well received.

As we need to be certain of the answer, let it be rephrased: "Who is Satan's equal?" Certainly not Jesus and possibly not even prince Michael, another angelic being. One of the names for God in the Old Testament is *El Shaddai*, "God Almighty". The *El* coupling is Hebrew for "God". Intrinsically, the angels MichaEL and GabriEL have in their being the very name, nature and character of God. On the other side, the names Lucifer, Abaddon (the "Destroyer"), and BeELzebub ("the dung god") are grossly inferior in name, nature and character.

Regrettably, this truth has not been firmly established in many circles. I was once at a conference on deliverance, and heard the keynote speaker say, "I've been accused of seeing a demon behind every bush. That's not true. There are at least two." He wasn't being funny; rather, he was trying to impress upon us the unrelenting attack waged against us, by a very real, very powerful enemy.

I don't dispute the point that he was trying to make. I do,

---

[19] A chart of names and Scripture references can be found in Appendix B.

however, want to bring some redemptive arithmetic to bear. Tradition holds that a third of the angels fell. So, if there are two demons behind every bush, that means there are four angels faithfully standing close by! This is precisely the message of 2 Kings 6:15–17. While the servant Gehazi makes coffee early one morning, he looks out of the window and becomes terrified, for he sees the enemy's horses and chariots surrounding them. *"Oh master, which way are we to turn?"* The prophet Elisha answers, *"Do not be afraid, for those on our side are more than those on theirs."* He then prays, *"Lord, open his eyes and let him see."* Gehazi is subsequently graced to see into the unseen realm, and *"saw the hills covered with horses and chariots of fire"*.

Though it's nearly lost in translation, Jesus is absolutely confident that *"those on our side are more than those on theirs"*. At His arrest, it's as bad as it gets – He turns to the chief priests, the temple guards and the elders and declares, *"This is your hour – when darkness reigns."* [20] When Peter impulsively tries to defend Jesus, slashing the servant's ear, Jesus says, *"Put up your sword. All who take the sword die by the sword. Do you suppose that I cannot appeal for help to my Father, and at once be sent more than twelve legions of angels?"* [21] Add to that statement some detail from the apostle John's account of the arrest: a "detachment" or "cohort" of soldiers arrests Jesus.[22] The Greek word is *speira*, a technical term for a tenth of a legion. A legion numbers 6,000 men.

So, against 600 armed soldiers, plus unnumbered temple guards, a scared fisherman draws his machete – not a proper sword – and Jesus thanks him for the good intentions, but declines the help: *"Do you suppose that I cannot appeal for help to my Father, and at once be sent more than twelve legions . . ."*. "Seventy-two thousand angels – Peter, do the math!"

---

[20] Luke 22:53.
[21] Matthew 26:52–53.
[22] John 18:3, 12.

While the origins of evil are shrouded in mystery, the Scriptures leave us with two absolute certainties:

1. THIS IS NOT A FAIR FIGHT, and
2. WE'RE NOT THE ONES AT RISK.

Depending on one's background and personal history, some of the material covered in this chapter may be new ground. It may also be the case that it's not just new theology; experientially, this may have been very unfamiliar territory. The following present-day accounts are offered to help bridge the gap between our understanding of the Scriptures and a secular and materialistic worldview that only sees angels when the Christmas tree decorations come out each year.

I have a friend who's a medical doctor. Dr. John[23] was raised as a believer, but one unschooled in the things of the Spirit. The supernatural, demons and warfare were not a part of his operative theology. That began to change when he served at a government hospital in Zaire. After two years he said, "I realized that beneath the veneer of Western sophistication there were realms of which I knew nothing." He returned to Canada in the middle '70's. One of his new patients was diagnosed with Multiple Personality Disorder (MPD), now called Dissociative Identity Disorder (DID). Ongoing involvement with this patient pitched my friend headlong into the world of the unseen realm and Dr. John is truly one of the pioneer caregivers to these tormented souls. With his patient's permission, he allowed me to read through a thick file of notes he has taken over the course of the care he has extended. I also listened to some of the interviews he audio taped. I transcribed the following exchanges.

An unnaturally deep and gravelly voice complains: "I hate

---

[23] His name has been changed.

coming to your office. I hate being here. I'm only here because an angel drags me here every time."

Minutes later, another distinctively different voice says, "Ask them to leave." My friend asked, "Who? Who do you want to leave?" The voice answers, "The bright ones."

As part of the ongoing care for this patient, she was moved into church-funded and administrated low-income housing. In one of the interviews, yet another voice makes it very clear how unhappy "it" is with the new arrangements. "I hate that place. There are too many angels around."

On another tape, one of the presenting personalities said, "I hate it here in your office. I'm leaving." Moments earlier, another distinct personality had just blasphemed and declared that it was more powerful than Christ; that what the Bible said was all lies and that there was no victory in Christ. (I needed clarification with what took place next on the tape. Dr. John said that though he has never seen an angel, he regularly asks that the Lord station an angel at the door of his office to guard all of the comings and goings.) As the patient started to leave, my friend said, "If you're going to go, you have to get past the angel first." A voice whined, "Tell him to get away." "No. You just finished saying that you were stronger than Christ and that there is no victory in Him." She went to push against the angel and while it looked as if she was pushing air aside, she was immediately catapulted across the room, hit the wall with a splat and slumped to the floor!

Those interviews left me praying, "Lord, open my eyes and let me see . . . "

Chapter 3

The Strongman
Has Been Bound

*"War in its highest aspects consists not in
an infinitive number of little events . . .
but of separate, great decisive events."*
(Carl von Clausewitz, *On the Nature of War*)[1]

✤ ✤ ✤

"You cannot defeat me, praying man!" the Strongman
bellowed. "You have no power. *I* have defeated *you!*"

"Strongman," Hank said in a firm and steady voice, "in
the name of Jesus, I rebuke you! I rebuke you and I bind
you!"

"You cannot defeat me!" the Strongman screamed, and
his demons hoped, or rather wished it were true.

"Be quiet and come out of him!" Hank ordered.

His words threw the demons against the wall and hit
the Strongman like a left hook.

"You're defeated, Strongman!" said Hank.

The Strongman began to shake. The demons in the
room could only cower.

---

[1] Carl von Clausewitz, *On the Nature of War*, Penguin Books, London, 1832, p. 91.
Clausewitz's work is considered one of the classics on the conduct of war.

The Strongman could take no more of this praying man's rebukes. He wilted. His sword dropped ... and the Strongman was gone.[2]

The passage cited is from one of the most gripping scenes in Peretti's novel, *This Present Darkness*. The Strongman, especially capitalized as a proper name, has intentional biblical allusions. Peretti took a great deal of licence in using the name and in so doing, strayed a very long way from the biblical context.

The strongman is referred to but once in all of Scripture, in the Beelzebub controversy.[3] In its context, Jesus had effortlessly delivered a blind mute from an afflicting spirit and the scribes respond with a most twisted accusation: *"He is possessed by Beelzebul ... He drives out demons by the prince of demons."*[4] It was not the scribes' brightest moment. Jesus reminds them of Logic 101: *"How can Satan drive out Satan? If a kingdom is divided against itself, that kingdom cannot stand ... and if Satan is divided and rebels against himself, he cannot stand, and that is the end of him."*[5] Jesus continues, *"On the other hand, no one can break into a strong man's house and make off with his goods unless he has first tied up the strong man; then he can ransack the house."*[6]

In setting the captive free – the demonized blind mute – the reign and rule of the Kingdom of God triumphantly divides, not itself, but the reign and rule of the prince of demons. Put another way, in casting out the demon, the King of kings despoils the prince's "princedom".

But Jesus says this can only take place once the strongman

[2] Frank Peretti, *This Present Darkness*, Crossway Books, Westchester, 1986, pp. 354–5, 357, 359, 370.

[3] Matthew 12:22–29; Mark 3:22–27; Luke 11:14–22.

[4] Mark 3:22.

[5] Mark 3:23–26.

[6] Mark 3:27.

has been bound. Traditional interpretation of this passage cites one of the Messianic prophecies in Isaiah as commentary:

> *"Can plunder be taken from warriors,*
> *or captives rescued from the fierce?*
>
> *But this is what the* Lord *says:*
>
> *'Yes, captives will be taken from warriors,*
> *and plunder retrieved from the fierce;*
> *I will contend with those who contend with you,*
> *and your children I will save . . . .*
> *Then all mankind will know*
> *that I, the* Lord, *am your Saviour,*
> *your Redeemer, the Mighty One of Jacob.' "*[7]

With these verses in hand, the declarations of the synagogue demoniac are all the more poignant: *"What do you want with us, Jesus of Nazareth? Have you come to destroy us? I know who You are – the Holy One of God."*[8]

Jesus literally muzzles the demon that interrupts His teaching, but later engages the faulty logic of the Beelzebub accusation by seizing the moment to counter with the strong-man story. He teaches by implication that the binding and disarming of Satan has preceded the plundering that takes place as He casts out demons. Jesus gives no indication as to where or when this binding or disarming has taken place; He merely implies that it has been accomplished.

Peretti's timeframe and hero, therefore, are all wrong: the strongman was bound two thousand years ago and not by a praying pastor, but by one Stronger than the strongman.[9]

---

[7] Isaiah 49:24–26, NIV.

[8] Mark 1:24.

[9] Luke 11:22.

Irenaeus was the first church father to elaborate a comprehensive doctrine of redemption. A bare-bones question directed his work: "For what reason did Christ come down from Heaven?" His bare-bones answer: "That He might kill sin, deprive death of its power and give life to man."[10] Irenaeus unpacks this summary statement by saying:

> "Man had been created by God that he might have life. Having lost life and having been harmed by the serpent, he was ... wholly abandoned to death ... but through the Second Man He bound the strongman and spoiled his goods, and annihilated death, bringing life to man who had become subject to death .... He who had taken man captive was himself taken captive by God and man who had been taken captive was set free from the bondage of condemnation."[11]

Irenaeus drew from a number of Scriptures, among them the Lord's teaching on the strongman, as well as Ephesians 4:8 (NKJV): "*When* [Christ] *ascended on high, He led captivity captive...* "[12] and 1 John 3:8: "*the Son of God appeared for the very purpose of undoing the devil's work.*" The word translated "undoing" is a very comprehensive one and can equally be rendered "destroy".[13] Irenaeus also employs Hebrews 2:14:

> "*By dying he might break the power of him who had death at his command, that is, the devil, and might liberate those who all their life had been in servitude through fear of death.*"

---

[10] Irenaeus, *Against Heresies*, III.18.7, Ante-Nicene Fathers, vol. 1, Hendrickson Pub., Peabody, Mass, 1994, p. 448.

[11] Irenaeus, *Against Heresies*, III.23.1, Ante-Nicene Fathers, vol. 1, Hendrickson Pub., Peabody, Mass, 1994, p. 455–6; quoted from Gustaf Aulen's translation, *Christus Victor*, SPCK, London, 1970, p. 20.

[12] NRSV, NKJV, KJV. NIV "captives in his train" suppresses the doubling of captivity.

[13] KJV, NKJV, NASB, NRSV, NET and NLT.

The Gospels continuously attest that the supernatural power of God at work through Jesus brought release, healing and restoration to individuals long tormented, distressed and fractured. The sufferer was relieved, the prisoner set free, evil undone. These were the consequences of His coming. But deliverance was not isolated and individuated. Jesus' exorcisms meant that a new age had dawned and in it, the powers of darkness were bound. The Kingdom of God had come. In Jesus there is a greater limiting, a greater binding of darkness than at creation. The first Adam was instructed to subdue the earth; the Second Adam subdued not only earth, but the spirit realm as well.

The casting out of demons was one dynamic aspect of the Lord's authoritative reign and rule and an irrefutable one. Jesus concluded the Beelzebub controversy with these words: *"If I drive out demons by the Spirit of God, then the kingdom of God has come upon you."* [14]

There are seven distinct accounts of deliverance recorded in the gospels and none of them give any evidence of an uncertain power struggle. Mention has already been made of the unclean spirit that interrupts Jesus in the synagogue; he is summarily rebuked, silenced and commanded to come out. [15] The blind and dumb demoniac is simply cured, his sight and speech restored. [16] The Gospel writers give the Gadarene demoniac's deliverance lengthy consideration, but the exorcism itself is not protracted. [17] The afflicting spirit is driven out of the dumb demoniac without a fuss [18] and the daughter of the Syrophenician woman is restored after an extended question and answer session. [19] (This is the only account of a long-distance

---

[14] Matthew 12:28, NIV.

[15] Mark 1:21–8; Luke 4:31–7.

[16] Matthew 12:22–23; Luke 11:14.

[17] Matthew 8:28–32; Mark 5:1–20; Luke 8:26–39.

[18] Matthew 9:32–33.

[19] Matthew 15:21–28; Mark 7:24–30.

deliverance, for the girl isn't present.) The evil spirit that afflicts the epileptic boy is no challenge for Jesus;[20] He has only to speak sternly to it and it leaves, and the boy is immediately healed. Lastly, to the woman with a spirit of infirmity, Jesus says only, *"You are rid of your trouble."* When He lays His hands on her, she is instantly delivered from her eighteen-year bondage, one which is attributed explicitly to Satan.[21]

In every case, Jesus is unquestionably in control of the situation and there is simply no contest, the outcome assured. The demons come out of their victims as supplicants rather than negotiators; they are certainly never combatants.[22] And when Jesus commissions His seventy-two disciples to proclaim the presence of the Kingdom of God and heal the sick, they do so like kids let loose in the proverbial candy store, reporting jubilantly that the *"demons submit to us in Your name."*[23] Jesus' literal response strikes an important contrast: He says, *"Do not rejoice that the spirits submit to you, but that your names are enrolled in heaven."*[24] Jesus would have His followers understand at least two things here: first, that their relationship with their heavenly Father is ever-more important than whatever authority they have over the powers of darkness; and second, if we're not having fun casting out demons, we're doing it wrongly!

A detailed study of the worst-case scenario makes it evidently clear that Jesus has indeed bound the strongman and is actively, intentionally despoiling his goods. By all accounts, Legion is the most demonized individual in all of Scripture. He is so

---

[20] Matthew 17:18; Mark 9:25; Luke 9:42.

[21] Luke 13:10–17.

[22] Robert Guelich, "Spiritual Warfare: Jesus, Paul and Peretti", *Pneuma*, Spring 1991, vol. 13:1, p. 40.

[23] Luke 10:17, NIV.

[24] Luke 10:20.

demonized his demons have demons! But he is only demon-ized. He is not "possessed". This recognition was but one of the many contributions John Wimber made in his groundbreaking book, *Power Healing*.[25] Most English Bibles unfortunately translate the Greek, *de-mon-idz-o-men-on* as "possessed". As we get many of our English words directly from the Greek – like "phobia" from *phobos* ("fear") – it is lamentable that translators don't simply use the word "demonized" as is done in the Spanish Bible, *endemoniados*.

Possession is a significant overstatement, for it implies ownership. It is appropriate for me to speak about possessing my Bible. It was a gift given to me by First Baptist Church in recognition of the completion of my doctorate. My name is in the flyleaf – I own it. But Satan and his demons possess nothing but their own evil. Repeatedly the Scriptures affirm, *"To the LORD belong the earth and everything in it, the world and all its inhabitants."*[26] To speak of demon "possession" is to give Satan undue honour and ownership of that which is not his. Language does define reality and if the devil is given more than is his due, it feeds our fears and deepens our insecurities. We compromise the sovereignty of God and end up with a very robust devil.

The demonized man known as Legion lived in the midst of death. He only felt at home in the cemetery. He was self-harming and manifested superhuman strength. One of the perverted distortions Legion suffered was that though so horribly bound, he was able to break the strongest of chains – but everything about his life changed when someone Stronger came. Legion also suffered another aspect of a flipped reality: he believed that the demons were his friends and that Jesus was his adversary. Lying voices convinced Legion that the Healer had come to torment him.

In the course of the deliverance, the demons *"implored Jesus*

---

[25] John Wimber, *Power Healing*, HarperCollins, San Francisco, 1987, p. 109.
[26] Exodus 19:5; Deuteronomy 10:14; Psalms 24:1; 50:12; 89:11.

not to send them out of the district."[27] This is one of the few
biblical texts that are championed by those teaching on
territorial spirits. But just as demons don't own a person,
neither do they own a place. Again, *"The earth is the Lord's and
all that is in it."*[28] While Legion's demons did not possess the
region, it is appropriate to speak of them as "familiar" spirits.
They counted the place as "Home sweet perverted home".
Regardless of whatever evil had been perpetrated and irrespec-
tive of what had been pledged, bought or covenanted, they had
no legal rights or grounds to the region. Jesus treats the
demons as squatters; they are evicted as illegal residents and
sent packing.

After the deliverance, ex-Legion is the picture of health,
sitting ... clothed and in his right mind."[29] He has assumed the
posture of a disciple; where he was once totally rebellious, he is
now teachable; where once he was naked and completely
alone, he is now socialized and in relationship; where he was
once crazy with torment, he is now sane and at peace. This
naked, suicidal maniac is so transformed that he is commissioned and sent forth as a passionate evangelist, telling his
townspeople of the grace he has experienced.[30]

For those still reticent to surrender the translated term
"possession", consider the following. Demon possession
implies absolute control, unaccountability and total victimization. In contrast, demonization means partial control or
influence over one or more areas of life. One of the greatest
spiritual heroes that ever lived, St. Antony of Padua, taught the
following when he preached on deliverance:

"If [demons] had any authority, they would not permit
one of us Christians to live .... To end our fear of them,

27 Mark 5:10.
28 1 Corinthians 10:26.
29 Mark 5:15.
30 Mark 5:19–20.

we ought to ponder this – the devil has no authority over swine, for, as it is written in the Gospel – they begged the Lord, saying, 'Send us into the swine.' But if they held no sway over the swine, how much less do they hold over people made in the image of God. We need, therefore, to fear God alone, holding them [the demons] in contempt and fearing them not at all."

This was not just rhetoric for Antony. One night he was beset by a demonic horde, made manifest in horrible, beastly form – lions, bears, leopards, bulls, serpents, scorpions and wolves.

> "Their ragings were fierce. But unmoved and even more watchful in his soul he lay there, and, as if mocking them, he said, 'If there were some power among you, it would have been enough for only one of you to come . . . . If you are able, and you did receive authority over me, don't hold back, but attack. But if you are unable, why, when it is vain, do you disturb me? For faith in our Lord is for us a seal and a wall of protection.'"[31]

Antony rose, made the sign of the cross, commanded the demons to depart and went back to sleep.

The following present-day stories are offered, in no way for dramatic effect. They are presented with a certain reticence, for the details could feed a twisted fascination with the darkness. Rather, the hope is that they demonstrate the realities considered thus far.

My doctor friend John extends care to another patient who is also MPD/DID. He met her in the early '80s. At the time she'd

---

[31] Athanasius, *The Life of Antony*, trans. Robert Gregg, Paulist Press, New York, 1980, pp. 53–54 and 38. Antony died in AD 356.

been admitted to the psychiatric ward of the local hospital and was being treated for clinical depression. The examining physician noted, "personality switching". The referral letter from a previously treating psychiatrist read: "Damaged goods – good luck." That was the professional, medical assessment.

As Dr. John slowly got to know this woman, it became apparent that trust was a huge issue for her. Initially she would hardly speak to him. My friend gradually, gently, directed conversation into the spiritual realm. He would also have praise tapes playing when she would come for her appointments. Dr. John was startled when the woman's voice and countenance changed markedly and a different "person" began shouting, "Stop it! We hate that music! Shutttt upppp!" At the end of another visit, he gave the woman a tract outlining the four spiritual laws. She brought it back on her next visit, shredded.

As part of her therapy, she was encouraged to keep a diary. I was allowed to look at it. Throughout, there are distinctly different types of writing and at times, it felt as though I was reading Legion's journal. Some of the text was flowing and distinctly feminine. Other passages were tight and constrained. Some script is block, other parts are written back-handedly. Another script is effusively vulgar. One passage was written in blood: "I will kill him." The "him" named is Dr. John.

After the session when they first discussed spiritual things, the dated entry reads, "Stay away from him. You are not to see him again."

Several months into the counselling the woman attempted suicide. Dr. John called on her in the psych ward. During the visit, he took out the Bible that was in the drawer of the bedside table. He asked if he could read something. He turned to Ephesians 6, *"We do not wrestle against flesh and blood, but against principalities, against powers, against the rulers of the darkness of this age . . . ".* John felt a chill come over him as he was reading. When he looked up from the Bible, she was in a catatonic state.

And then a deep, guttural voice growled, "She cannot hear what you are saying. She hears what we allow her to hear."

Over the next months, several experiments followed. The woman had no difficulty whatsoever reading out loud from the newspaper or a passage from a *Readers Digest*. If she read Scripture however, she would gloss over the name of Jesus and never read the words "Satan" or "the devil". When she was told, "You're not reading all the words," she replied, "I'm reading exactly what I'm seeing."

My friend invited her come to church with him. She did so very reluctantly and was restless throughout the service. At her medical appointment later that week she said that she hated going: "After the first song, I wanted to stand up and scream, 'It's lies, it's all lies.'"

Dr. John slowly learned some of the details of the woman's history. She had been sexually abused by her mother from infancy until the age of nine. She wasn't aware of any overt occult involvement on her parents' part, yet one of the voices repeatedly said, "She will never be free. She is ours."

In sessions in the clinic office, distorted voices regularly spoke: "We have her; we're going to get you. Your armour won't stand up. You will pay for interfering in what has been determined. All the forces of hell will come against you and your family and you will pay." Dr. John countered, "The blood of Jesus is my protection and [the patient's name] is marching toward freedom, and you cannot prevent it." A guttural voice countered, "We can and we will."

Ongoing intimidation was a characteristic subject of conversation. This patient would point to my friend's family photos and unnatural voices would declare, "They will all die." During one session, the woman relayed the previous night's dream: the doctor's house had burned to the ground and his family had burned to death. His Bible was the only thing that remained – it was mangled and thrown out on the driveway. By the end of the dream even it was destroyed, for it spontaneously combusted. My friend was again threatened: "Your armour will not protect you."

Eventually the woman became a Christian. A twenty-four-hour prayer team had been recruited to minister her deliverance; at four am she prayed, "I confess Jesus as my Lord and Saviour and I want nothing to do with the darkness. I ask Jesus that by the power of Your blood, send all the black angels away and never let them return."

Dr. John confessed that her deliverance was more a case of her own declaration than any ministry she received. Several years of personality integration and spiritual growth have followed, punctuated by moments of breakthrough.

No matter how dark or despairing, no matter how tormented or twisted a human life can become, no matter how powerful the lies and pervasive the deceptions, the word of the Lord resounds: *"I will build my church; and the gates of hell shall not prevail against it."*[32]

The word "prevail" is also translated "overcome" or "conquer".[33] It is a compound Greek word and has as its root the word "strength" – the same root word that is used of the strongman.[34] Just as Jesus is stronger than the strongman, He declares that His church will be stronger than all the works of the devil. Jesus is absolutely certain: this is an unfair contest. Satan has been mastered and his holdings are at risk. Eugene Peterson does a good job paraphrasing in *The Message*: Jesus purposes to establish a *"church so expansive with energy that not even the gates of hell will be able to keep it out"*.

---

[32] Matthew 16:18, KJV.

[33] NIV, REB.

[34] *Kat-is-ku-sou-sin*, Matthew 16:18; *is-ku-rou*, Matthew 12:29; *Theological Dictionary of the New Testament*, vol. III, Gerhard Kittel, Eerdmans, 1965, pp. 397–402.

Chapter 4

Deliverance by Dishes

*"It got so bad, I was afraid I **wasn't** going to die."*
(Humberto Fernandez, *Heroin*) [1]

✤ ✤ ✤

Kent Martin and his wife Mary Alice have been the directors of Betel of Britain since 1996. Betel is an international association of churches founded in Madrid, Spain. Their ministry mandate is to care for substance abusers and the marginalized. Betel of Britain presently has four residential communities. The main centre is located in south-east Birmingham and Betel in the UK has helped over 2,500 men and women. As they have ministered to some of humanity's darkest and most desperate, they estimate that only ten per cent have had overt occult experience. However, the majority – eighty per cent – would have an acute awareness of supernatural oppression at work in their lives. As I have interviewed dozens of those who count Betel as their new home, time and again they would confess that as they were about to inject, they would stare at the needle and feel that, "Something came over me. Something was driving me in my self-destruction."

Kent summarized: "Unlike most of society, it's not at all hard for the guys to believe that there's a devil. They may not believe in God, but they sure do believe in the devil."

I asked him to clarify. "I don't think someone can get very far

---

[1] Humberto Fernandez, *Heroin*, Hazelden, 1998, p. 45.

into drugs without demonic influence. Once they've penetrated the edges of the drug culture and find themselves in the vortex, they come into the grip of the ancient quest for power and control. This is the very root of witchcraft, the piercing of the veil of the spiritual world. An end-use addict has entered into a realm that is beyond the natural. Especially with the psychedelics, LSD and the like, it is a very spiritual experience, but not in a good way. The paranoia is the cost of that spiritual penetration."

I asked Kent and Mary Alice about their experience of deliverance ministry. Given that the guys and girls at Betel had come from such overtly dark histories, I was struck by their answers.

Kent said, "We don't go beating the bushes for demons – when they arise, we deal with them. And to be honest, it's not terribly often, which, when you think of it, is good news, given the fact that the guys we deal with have given the enemy open access to their lives, spiritually, physically and emotionally. But what's interesting is that you'd think we'd have to deal with deliverance more often than we do. It seems that the healing and the dispelling of the enemy rarely happens instantaneously, but over a process, over time, as God fills up their lives."

Mary Alice added, "Most of the warfare we conduct is in the truth realm, far more than in the power realm. Spiritual warfare for us is a way of life and what we're constantly doing is exposing the lies that hold the guys captive. That's what really delivers them over the long run.

"Most of the guys are brought to wholeness without dramatic deliverance. The talons of oppression are released by truth and worship empowering change, far more than the raw power of dramatic deliverance. More often than not, the demonic lifts, more than it's 'cast out'. That's the case most of the time, for most of the guys."

In March 2006, I returned to Birmingham, England, to preach at Betel's national conference. I met and subsequently interviewed a man who was brought to wholeness most un-dramatically, for he is quick to say that his deliverance came while washing dishes!

Billy[2] had a most violent past. He's been stabbed sixteen times. He has a dent in his skull where someone clobbered him with a hammer. He has a slash across his forehead from the business end of a machete. He's been shot four times – he had robbed two drug dealers of £50,000 in cash and several kilos of heroin, and several days later thugs in disguise came crashing through the door of his house, and Margaret Thatcher and George Bush started shooting.

He has given far more than he has received.

Billy was raised in Leeds and came from a very poor family. His mom worked three jobs, but it was never enough, or good enough. Billy's father was a violent alcoholic and made their home life miserable. As a young boy, Billy tried to be the dad of the family. He'd shoplift to provide for his mom and siblings. After being arrested repeatedly he was sent away to one care home after another. Thieving and violence were his only skills. By the age of fourteen, the magistrates had to come down to the jail cell to remand him in custody because he was so wild they couldn't get him up to the docks. On his release, the wrong people noticed his fearlessness in a fight and he was welcomed into the drug world.

"As a young lad, I really envied the guys in the big cars with their fast living – not knowing that to get there and stay there everybody was stabbing each other in the back – literally. That's the way I got there – by taking people out."

He progressed through petty pushing by stabbing and shooting intermediaries to get to the top. He felt no remorse for any of the pain he caused. "I didn't have a heart. I could go

---

[2] His name has been changed.

out and shoot someone and not even blink. I'd do them and go and have a nice meal."

He was soon the head of his own gang, moving street deals involving "a load" of heroin. For the buzz, he continued with armed robberies, even though he didn't need the money. His abandon to violence followed him in and out of prison. He is forty years old and has spent twenty years in prison. He's been beaten repeatedly by prison guards but admitted, "Nine times out of ten I probably deserved it. They're not going to let me knock one of their mates or a police officer around. I knew what was coming, but I'd get it in anyways." A number of times he needed to be so restrained he was chained to the wall, "like in *Papillon*".

He has held both prison guards and prisoners hostage; his behaviour was such that he spent much of the time in segregation, for a total of three years on one sentence. Much of that time he was under three-man unlock – for the single hour of twenty-four in which he was let out of his cell, three guards in full body armour would accompany him to his meals or exercise.

His heroin addiction got the better of him and things quickly began to unravel. It wasn't long before he was on the streets, shooting people for 300 quid. He went "from eating in the top restaurants in town to eating out of the best skips".[3]

One afternoon, he had just committed a robbery and was in the town centre of Leeds.[4] He was sitting on a step, his big butcher knife strapped to his side, and a big bag of drugs in his pocket. A police van pulled up and he thought, "There's going to be a battle here; someone's going to get hurt – probably me in the end, but they'll remember the afternoon." To his great surprise, one of the officers came up to him and said, "It's your lucky day – we're on our dinner break." Billy turned to leave and entered the first door that was open. It was a Christian

---

[3] Garbage dumpsters.
[4] Names have been changed throughout this story.

drop-in, the Daily Bread. He stayed and began talking to one of the volunteers, Enid. She knew Billy Glover, the pastor of the Betel Birmingham church and she told him stories of guys that had found a place where their lives got turned around. She paused, took a long look at him and said, "You've got the saddest looking face I've ever seen." That unsettled Billy, for he was convinced no one saw behind his emotional mask. He went to leave, but just before he reached the door, he turned round and pulled out his knife. Enid started praying aggressively in tongues. Billy thought, "What the . . . ?" He said, "Look, I haven't come to rob ya – I've come to give you this." He passed her his knife and left.

As soon as he got outside, he thought, "Oh no, what have I done?" He felt naked. He was never outside without his "tool".

One of the other volunteers, Charles, had followed him outside and asked if he wanted help. That was something Billy had never experienced before. He looked around and something inside broke. He said, "Yeah." "OK," said the man, "Meet me here tomorrow morning, nine o'clock." Billy didn't go at nine; he went at eleven, hoping that there'd be no one to meet him. There was – Charles told him that God had said he was to stay until Billy came. Billy thought, "How is it God is suddenly involved in any of this?" Charles took him up to the office and phoned Betel.

Billy knew nothing was going to happen. He had just been released from prison, but just before he left, he had vengefully blinded another prisoner. He had a court date pending. When he explained things over his admissions interview, he was told he couldn't come to Betel until that was all sorted. He hung up the phone, told Charles the news and Charles said, "Let's pray." Billy then felt surrounded and as a quickly assembled group laid hands on him, it sounded to Billy like they'd all gone mad.

Moments later the phone rang. Mary Alice, the co-director of Betel was calling back. She asked a few more questions and said that he could come. The next day, Billy arrived at Betel, but got there "rattling". He wanted them to see what they were getting, so was already into his heroin withdrawal. His attitude was deplorable. He continuously swore at those trying to help him settle in; he refused to go to devotions or make his bed.

"I wanted one of them to call it on. If they'd just lose it with me, I could justify letting them have it. But they wouldn't. By the second day I was getting sick and these guys were wiping up my vomit." He let them know what he thought of their kindnesses: "I explicitly told them where they should go. I was being so horrible about them being so nice," he told me.

Once through his detox, Billy was disciplined continuously. "The first four months I was in Kent's house more than Kent. The seven months I stayed, I was on dishes for five of them. But even though I was being horrible, in my heart I respected these guys. As I watched Kent and Wayne and Paul, the way they lived, the way they dealt with things, I thought, 'Wow, that's integrity. That's what's been missing.'"

One day Billy lost his temper with one of the leaders and backhanded him across the face. He was told he had to leave Betel.

"I was gutted. I didn't show it, but I was really gutted. Back on the streets, I missed Wayne Wood's correction. I thought of all the times I'd said 'I hate that guy. He's always on my back.' I was always in Mark Potter's office. He'd be on me for my attitude and then he'd pray for me, asking God to bring the rubbish to the surface so He could deal with it. You know what? I missed them. I missed the correction and even the discipline. There is an aura about Betel. Not an 'aura' – it's the love, the care, even when I was getting corrected. I'd come into the office to get it in the neck and I'd go out bigger than when I came in! Happier, even though I just got another two months of dishes.

"When I came back, I made a pact with God. I know you can't make a pact with God, but I did, 'cause I figured I was still new so I could get away with it. 'If You can change my heart, my arrogance and the violence, I'll do all that I can to follow You. I know it's real what these guys have and I just want to have even a little bit of it in my heart. You do that and I'll do everything I can to give everything back to You, to serve You.' And God said, 'OK.' "

Watching Billy over the course of the weekend, it was hard for me to imagine his past. He is gentle, soft-spoken and repeatedly demonstrated a pastor's heart. When I interviewed him, I asked, "What happened to the anger, the rage, and the hatred that had you chained to the wall?"

Billy took a deep breath and grinned. "Only God knows. I don't. I just felt this peace that came around me as soon as I came through the doors of Betel. I was still angry, but when I was putting my defences up, I'd look around and never forget that these were the guys that were cleaning up my sick, and cleaning me up when I couldn't get to the toilet. When I'd get corrected, I'd always be told that they could 'see beyond'. I don't know what they were seeing, but it sounded better than what I was living!

"I knew that my mom loved me, but she never ever told me that. When I got to Betel it was one of the first things that Kent told me – 'We love you, man.' And he gave me a hug. Those first few days especially, I was a proper pain in the bum, but he knew my name, he'd sit down and talk decently to me and he'd make me feel welcome. All the while, I'm trying to put up barriers – I didn't know how to receive the love. The only thing that made a difference in my life was the love and the care and the correction. I never knew how to give love or receive it. That was the fear factor that drove me away from here the first time. That's why I left, why I slapped a guy. The love scared me. Genuine love. I'd never let anyone in and I just felt too vulnerable. I couldn't handle it. Kent had told me that my rage was like trying to hold a beach ball under water.

Eventually it was going to pop up. Praise God, I only slapped the guy.

"But it was strange. On the streets, I could shoot a guy and not feel nothing. As soon as I had given the lad just a little slap, it was the first time I had the feeling that I'd done something wrong. 'I've let Kent down, I've let Mary Alice down.' And then I thought, 'Where is all this coming from?'

"I was out for sixteen months and I went to work in the drop-in café where my life first started to turn around. But I thought I knew everything. I was telling people like myself that they needed to get themselves to Betel, that it was their only hope.

"My mom died suddenly and I was straight back to the gear. Like a dog, I went straight back to my own vomit. I had a punch-up with a guy and was watching telly later that night. There was a story on the news about a shooting death just down the street from where I lived and I heard in my heart God telling me I needed to go back to Betel, or that would be me.

"I didn't listen. Instead, I went out to the pub. Late that night, an old mate of mine came up and told me that there were a load of guys around, looking for me. They had guns and they were going to waste me. I told him I didn't care. Having just lost my mom, I wanted to die. God spoke to me again and said, 'No, you've got a family in Betel. They love you and they want you back.' But I was trying to blank it out.

"I fought with myself all night long and the next day, I gave in and came back to Betel. Once I got settled back in, the leaders asked to see me in the office. I used to call them the Christian SAS, so I knew I was in for it. Five of them were standing there and basically said, 'You need to put up and shut up. We're not having the attitude any more.' I went back to my room and got it settled. This is where I want to be.

"The next few months were really hard. Everybody was on me for everything, nipping it in the bud. And I just kept humbling myself. I got some help too. I was working gardens one day and Mark asked me to move sixty $3' \times 2'$ cement flagstones from one end of a big garden to the other. No sooner did I get the last one moved, when Mark comes over, and says, 'Sorry, bring them back.'

"I can look back on it now and see that it wasn't the flagstones that needed to be moved, it was my attitude. He was looking for my reaction. Part of me wanted to break one of the flagstones over his head! I knew that attitude had only got me more time in a prison cell, so I had to totally humble myself. That was a huge breakthrough for me. In that moment, I made a choice.

"The passage in Romans 8:26 is a Scripture I always turn back to [Billy paraphrased]: 'the Holy Spirit hears your sighs and your groans, and gives them to God as eloquent prayers.' The first time I read that scripture, I thought 'how many times have I sat in a prison cell and just been at the end of it, and cried out, 'God there must be something more than this.' The Holy Spirit has taken those words and given them to God as such an eloquent prayer. And God's heard those prayers, time and again.

"That day in the garden, I asked God for help. I'd only ever had friends through fear – I didn't ever really have a family – and I didn't want to lose the guys in Betel. Guys that were correcting me, the guy that I'd threatened – they were the first ones to tell me they loved me when they heard that my brother died. Mark just came up and gave me a hug. That really touched something – it made me say, 'God I really want to try my best to honour what I said I'd do.' And it's like the air's been let out of the beach ball. The rage is gone. I still have to work on my attitude, but the anger's gone."

Billy was recently arrested for gun-running crimes he'd committed over a decade ago. He apologized to the officers saying, "You'll have to forgive me. I'm really struggling. This is the first time I've ever told the truth to a policeman. It might seem that I'm wavering, but I'm used to lying." Knowing of the details of Billy's past criminal record, the officers were very impressed with the transformation they witnessed in him.

Billy told me later, "I didn't want to hold anything back. God was telling me that I couldn't be ministering to any of the other guys if I didn't show my full hand. And it was a good thing that I did – the police knew everything I'd done anyways.

"I'm a 'responsible' now and I'm learning to correct the guys with love. Just like I got corrected. I want to thank God for all that He's done in me and I just can't find the ways.

"Having survived all the stabbings, the shootings, the hammer blows to my head and the machete in the forehead, I know God's got great plans for me, and I want to be the great man of God He wants me to be."

I sent the edited transcript of my interview to Kent so that he could verify the details of Billy's story. He did so and then added these closing words to his email:

"To know Billy now is, as you described it, to understand God's 'accelerated grace' incarnate. It's been spiritual alchemy – a lump of lead quickly transmuted into finest gold – so much more than a gradual transformation. The change defies explanation apart from supernatural deliverance. He entered foul-mouthed, rude, cocky and breathing violent threats. Thirteen months later – no exaggeration – he's among the hungriest for God. He's humble, respectful and deeply grateful.

"As to his future, I believe we'll see him serving God in Betel the rest of his life. Billy is custom built to take on a city for Christ, Betel-style. He's a born leader and now has a shepherd's heart. He's full of gritty, street-wit, but has a serious-minded love for the broken of this world."

Chapter 5

War and Worship

"War is a matter of vital importance, the province of life or death;
the road to survival or ruin. It is mandatory
that it be thoroughly studied."
(Sun Tzu, *The Art of War*)[1]

✠ ✠ ✠

In the Old Testament, the recurrent theme of holy war is a
near-continuous one, often with disturbingly bloody, ruthless
and gruesome outcomes. Israel's enemies are not overtly
demonic spirits, but rather, hostile neighbours and political
rivals. As unsettling as the battle accounts are, there is clear
revelation that the warfare is nevertheless spiritual, for it is the
Lord who delivers the enemy into Israel's hands.[2] He is Himself
the warrior[3] and it is He who overthrows those who oppose
Him and His people.

Moses tells the terrified Israelites, *"Have no fear; stand firm and*
see the deliverance that the LORD will bring you this day; for as sure as
you see the Egyptians now, you will never see them again. The LORD
will fight for you."[4] It is declared repeatedly that it is not Israel's
military might, be it numbers or armaments, that wins the day.
Rather, it is as Joshua reminded Israel, *"The LORD has driven out*
great and powerful nations before you .... One of you can rout a

---

[1]   Sun Tzu, *The Art of War*, trans. Samuel Griffith, Oxford, 1963, p. 63.
[2]   Joshua 2:24; 6:2, 16; Judges 3:28; 1 Samuel 23:4; 1 Kings 20:28 etc.
[3]   Exodus 15:3, 7.
[4]   Exodus 14:13.

thousand, because the LORD *your God fights for you.*"[5] For this reason, anyone who is afraid or has lost heart is dismissed from the Lord's army, for "*his faint-heartedness may affect his comrades.*"[6]

Given this same leave, two-thirds of Gideon's men abandon him, yet the Lord is most insistent: "*Those with you are more than I need to deliver Midian into their hands: Israel might claim the glory for themselves and say that it is their own strength that has given them the victory.*"[7] Jonathan also knows that "*nothing can stop* [the Lord] *from winning a victory, by many or by few*".[8] This very assurance empowers young David to take victory from Goliath and the Philistines, for "*the battle is the Lord's.*"[9] And be it Joshua's praise marching around Jericho, or Gideon's remnant armed only with torch and trumpet, it is the Lord who wins the day, supernaturally.

King Hezekiah inspires his military commanders with precisely this truth: "*Be strong; be brave. Do not let the king of Assyria or the rabble he has brought with him strike terror or panic into your hearts, for we have more on our side than he has. He has human strength; but we have the* LORD *our God to help us and to fight our battles.*"[10] It is no empty rhetoric, for the Lord sends a single angel to cut down every fighting man in the Assyrian camp.[11]

Because it is the Lord who goes "*forth as a warrior, a soldier roused to the fury of battle ...* [to] *triumph over His foes...*"[12] Isaiah repeatedly warns against those who "*rely upon horses, who put their trust in chariots ... but do not look to the Holy One of Israel.*"[13] The prophet is insistent: the people of God must

---

[5] Joshua 23:9–10.
[6] Deuteronomy 20:1–4, 8.
[7] Judges 7:2–3.
[8] 1 Samuel 14:6.
[9] 1 Samuel 17:45, 47.
[10] 2 Chronicles 32:7–8.
[11] 2 Chronicles 32:20–21.
[12] Isaiah 42:13.
[13] Isaiah 31:1; 22:8–11.

attend to a warfare of worship: *"In repentance and rest is your salvation, in quietness and trust is your strength."*[14] Similarly, the psalmist declares that it is the Lord who *"puts an end to war: he breaks the bow, he snaps the spear, he burns the shields in the fire."*[15] God's people are very clearly recruited in the fight, but the marching orders are otherworldly: *"be still and know that I am God."*[16]

The most detailed account of holy war is buried deep in 2 Chronicles. Jehoshaphat is king of Judah and like his father, he obeyed the commandments and sought the guidance of the Lord.[17] Under his righteous rule, the nation prospered; Jehoshaphat built fortresses and store-towns, and maintained a standing army of over a million seasoned troops.[18]

His peaceful reign was disturbed as the Moabites, the Ammonites and the Meunites assembled to make war on him. When the news of their impending attack reached Jehoshaphat, he did not rely on his military prowess, but immediately *"resolved to seek guidance of the* LORD, *and proclaimed a fast for all Judah"*.[19] His prayer concludes: *"Judge them, God our God, for we have not the strength to face this great host which is invading our land; we do not know what we ought to do, but our eyes look to you."*[20]

The Spirit of the Lord then came on Jahaziel and he began to prophesy: *"This is the word of the* LORD *to you: Do not fear or be dismayed by this great horde, for the battle is in God's hands, not yours. Go down to engage them tomorrow ... [but] it is not you who will fight this battle; stand firm and wait, and you will see the deliverance worked by the* LORD *for you."*[21] Jehoshaphat and the

---

14 Isaiah 30:15, NIV.
15 Psalm 46:9.
16 Psalm 46:10, NIV.
17 2 Chronicles 17:3–4.
18 2 Chronicles 17:14–19.
19 2 Chronicles 20:3.
20 2 Chronicles 20:12.
21 2 Chronicles 20:15–17.

people responded by prostrating themselves before the Lord, while the Levites stood and praised the Lord *"with mighty voice"*.

The next day, Jehoshaphat assembled the people and reminded them: *"Hold firmly to your faith in the* LORD *your God and you will be upheld."* With that the king's battle strategy is initiated: he assembles a worship team to *"praise the splendour of the Lord's holiness."* There follows one of the most under-stated declarations of Scripture: *"They marched out before the armed troops, singing...."*[22]

It is also followed by one of the most decisive victories recorded in Scripture. As the shouts of praise resounded, *"Give thanks to the* LORD, *for his love endures for ever,"* the Ammonites, Moabites and men of Seir were not only defeated; they had become so confused, *"they savagely attacked one another".*[23] When it was all over, there was so much booty to be collected it took King Jehoshaphat and his men three days to plunder the fallen armies, and on the fourth day they formally renamed the battlefield. No longer was it the wilderness of Tekoa. From that day forward, it was known as *"the valley of Berakah* [the valley of Blessing] *for the* LORD *had given them cause to triumph over their enemies".*[24]

✤ ✤ ✤

The Hebrew words for war occur over two hundred and seventy times in the Old Testament. In the New Testament, references to war diminish significantly. Under *Pax Romana* – "the Peace of Rome" – Palestine and the Near East prospered. Jesus was born at the height of the Roman Empire and while there were local insurrections during His lifetime and that of the early Church, there were no major military battles.

There are two Greek words that are translated as either "war" or "warfare". The predominant one, *polemos*, is used in

---

22 2 Chronicles 20:19–21.

23 2 Chronicles 20:23.

24 2 Chronicles 20:24–27.

the New Testament only twenty-five times. One reference is found in Luke 14:31: a king must count the cost before going to war. Paul uses *polemos* in 1 Corinthians 14:8, *"If the trumpet-call is not clear, who will prepare for battle?"* The heroes of faith *"became mighty in war,* [and] *put foreign enemies to flight".*[25] Five occurrences are found in the prophetic warning Jesus issues to the disciples of nations raging against nations, of *"wars and rumours of war".*[26] Fifteen times *polemos* is used of the war that will be waged in Heaven – the final, eschatological war that precedes the creation of the new heaven and earth, the "war that ends all wars".[27] One example will suffice: the beast and his horde *"will wage war on the Lamb, but the Lamb will conquer them".*[28]

Polemos is used twice in the context of warring appetites. The apostle James asks, *"Where do wars and fights come from among you? Do they not come from your desires that war in your members?"*[29]

The second Greek word for war or warfare is *strateia*. It is employed five times in the context of godly character. James uses it with *polemos* in the verses cited above. Similarly, the apostle Paul names the internal conflict that rages, *"the members of my body, waging war against the law of my mind".*[30] Paul also encourages his beloved Timothy to persevere in the service of the Gospel, to pursue godly character, to be pure in conscience, and in all of this, to *"fight the good fight"*, which the KJV translates literally: *"war a good warfare".*[31] In much the same way the apostle Peter admonishes his friends to keep themselves pure and undefiled and guard themselves against the *"bodily desires which make war on the soul".*[32]

---

[25]   Hebrews 11:34, NASB.
[26]   Matthew 24:6–7; Mark 13:7; Luke 21:9.
[27]   See Revelation 11:7; 12:7; 13:7; 19:20–21.
[28]   Revelation 17:14.
[29]   James 4:1–2, NKJV.
[30]   Romans 7:23, NASB.
[31]   1 Timothy 1:18.
[32]   1 Peter 2:11.

The fifth use of *strateia* requires careful consideration, for it is frequently plucked from its context, pressed into the service of spiritual warfare and seriously over-worked. Under the umbrella of this single text it is popularly taught that we wage war against "strongholds of fear, worry, bitterness, anger, shame, control, etc."[33] Because the passage is so inappropriately misinterpreted, a careful study of the text follows.

The NIV translates 2 Corinthians 10:3–5:

> *"For though we live in the world, we do not wage war as the world does. The weapons we fight with are not the weapons of the world. On the contrary, they have divine power to demolish strongholds. We demolish arguments and every pretension that sets itself up against the knowledge of God, and we take captive every thought to make it obedient to Christ."*

A literal translation of verse 3 would read: "In flesh – *sarki* – we are walking; not according to flesh – *sarka* – we war." The NIV takes considerable liberty in interpreting *sarx*, the root of the word, as "world". In Greek, that word is *cosmos*. Verse 4 is similarly mistranslated: we do not fight with *"weapons of the world"*; rather, *"the weapons of our warfare are not fleshly"*.

Until the resurrection, life must necessarily be lived *"in the flesh"*, but never *"according to the flesh"*. Rather, in Christ, we live *"according to the Spirit"*. Life cannot be other than in the flesh; "it would be as impossible as bodiless existence".[34] The flesh is only bad when we try to build our lives on it.[35] As Tevye says in *The Fiddler on the Roof*, "We are in the mud, but not of the mud."

---

[33] Chester and Betsy Kylstra, *An Integrated Approach to Biblical Healing Ministry*, Sovereign World, Tonbridge, 2003, p. 114.

[34] James Dunn, *The Theology of the Apostle Paul*, T. & T. Clark, Edinburgh, 1998, p. 68.

[35] Eduard Schweizer, *Theological Dictionary of the New Testament*, vol. vii, Eerdmans, Grand Rapids, 1971, p. 135.

All of this needs to be put in its larger context. In the Corinthian letters, Paul has to contend for both his apostolic authority and his understanding of the Gospel, particularly with respect to the centrality of the cross. This is especially the case in 2 Corinthians 10–13. The apostle gently declares his concerns: *"I am afraid that just as Eve was deceived by the serpent's cunning, your minds may somehow be led astray from your sincere and pure devotion to Christ."*[36]

False apostles had criticized Paul's authority, in part by finding fault with his physical afflictions. He makes no apologies; in fact, he makes them something of a boast. *"If distress is our lot, it is the price we pay for your consolation and your salvation."*[37] As to the weapons of his warfare, they are not sword, spear and shield, but *"weapons of righteousness"*. He counters the attacks that come against him with *"steadfast endurance . . . innocent behaviour and grasp of truth . . . patience and kindliness . . . gifts of the Holy Spirit . . . unaffected love, by declaring the truth, by the power of God"*.[38]

The war he fights is fought on the battlefield of doctrine and character, for Paul's enemies are those "super-apostles" who teach *"another Jesus . . . a spirit different from the Spirit already given to you, or a gospel different from the gospel you have already accepted"*.[39] Over and against the super-apostles' proud triumphalism and self-serving demands, Paul again commends the Corinthians to *"the Christ who, far from being weak with you, makes his power felt among you. True, he died on the cross in weakness, but he lives by the power of God; so you will find that we who share his weakness shall live with him by the power of God"*.[40] This is what Paul means by demolishing strongholds.

---

[36]   2 Corinthians 11:3, NIV.

[37]   2 Corinthians 1:6.

[38]   2 Corinthians 6:4–7.

[39]   2 Corinthians 11:4–5.

[40]   2 Corinthians 13:3–4.

In summary, warfare in the Old Testament is conducted against foreign enemies. Attack comes from armed soldiers, not demons. And short of the end times, there is no New Testament use of either *polemos* or *strateia* for a spiritual war that engages believers directly with the demonic. As pervasive as the term "spiritual warfare" has become over the last two decades, the phrase itself is not found anywhere in the Scriptures.

Further, neither Satan nor the demonic receive any extended discourse anywhere in the Scriptures. He and his horde are given only passing references. In the Gospels there are a mere seventeen separate references to the devil, however he is named.

The tempter comes to Jesus in the wilderness and unsuccessfully tries Him with three temptations.[41] In the Lord's Prayer, Jesus taught the disciples to pray deliverance from the evil one's craft.[42] Twice Jesus portrays the evil one as the farmer's nemesis, snatching the seed before it can produce a harvest[43] and planting thistles among the wheat.[44] Once Jesus openly rebukes Satan's efforts to interfere in His Messianic destiny[45] and Peter and the other disciples are warned of Satan's plans to sift them like wheat.[46] In a confrontation with the Pharisees, Jesus tells them that their father is the devil, a murderer, a liar and the father of lies.[47] Only once does Jesus explicitly attribute physical sickness to Satan,[48] though healing is often the consequence of deliverance.[49]

On six separate occasions Jesus declared Satan's demise; He had bound the strongman and was despoiling his holdings;[50]

---

[41] Matthew 4:1–11; Mark 1:12–13; Luke 4:1–13.
[42] Matthew 6:13.
[43] Matthew 13:19; Mark 4:15; Luke 8:12.
[44] Matthew 13:39.
[45] Matthew 16:23; Mark 8:33.
[46] Luke 22:31.
[47] John 8:44.
[48] Luke 13:16.
[49] Matthew 12:22; Luke 11:14 etc.
[50] Matthew 12:22–29; Mark 3:23–27; Luke 11:17–22.

while the disciples cast out demons, He watched as Satan fell like lightning;[51] and as an aside, mentioned that eternal fire was prepared for the devil and his angels.[52] Jesus assured His distraught disciples that the prince of this world was not only soon to be driven out,[53] but that he had no rights over Jesus[54] and that he already stood condemned.[55] There is also threefold witness to Satan's influence propelling Judas to betray Jesus.[56]

In all of these references, the work of Satan is adversarial, the living out of his literal name, the Adversary. None of these accounts employ military imagery or warfare language to describe Satan, his works, or the deliverances. Though the devil is once referred to as the enemy,[57] the context is that of personal harassment, not military aggression. In the wilderness, Jesus is only tempted; there is no battle fought; Satan certainly poses no threat to Jesus.

The apostle Paul writes very little about Satan and even less about demons or evil spirits. He makes only five references to the demonic; four of those are in the context of food and drink offered to demons;[58] the other is a future reference to the time when weak believers will *"surrender their minds to subversive spirits and demon-inspired doctrines"*.[59]

Paul names Satan ten times and refers to the devil another five. As with Jesus, the apostle treats Satan only as an adversarial enemy.[60] Through lack of self-control, believers *"may be tempted by Satan"*, and give way to lust or anger.[61]

---

[51] Luke 10:18.
[52] Matthew 25:41.
[53] John 12:31.
[54] John 14:30.
[55] John 16:11.
[56] John 6:70; 13:2, 27.
[57] Matthew 13:25.
[58] 1 Corinthians 10:20–21.
[59] 1 Timothy 4:1.
[60] 2 Thessalonians 2:4.
[61] 1 Corinthians 7:5; Ephesians 4:27; 1 Timothy 5:15.

Satan tries to harden the heart through unforgiveness;[62] he misleads,[63] impedes,[64] traps,[65] and harasses.[66] Nowhere in Paul's writings are believers encouraged to bind or defeat Satan. Rather they are assured that God will soon crush Satan beneath their feet.[67]

By way of contrast, the destructive forces most at work in the believer's life are death (cited fifty-six times), sin (fifty-four times in Romans alone, eighty-nine times in total), and the flesh (ninety-one times, though not all of these references have corruptive consequence).[68] And while Paul uses *pneuma* ("spirit") over one hundred fifty times, only two carry malevolent overtones.[69]

There is nothing of two opposing cosmic forces at war with one another in the heart, life or ministry of the believer. As Paul understands the work of the devil, he is only a potential threat to the believer's intimate relationship with God. Our adversary's methods nevertheless must be taken very seriously and will be given detailed consideration in following chapters.

In the New Testament, Satan is never blamed for inhibiting someone from entering the Kingdom, though the Pharisees are. Jesus never attributes sinful behaviour like anger, lust, broken marriages, murder or greed to demonic spirits. Rather, personal sin is the culprit and has its source in the depths of the human heart.[70] Neither Jesus nor Paul name "spirits of rebellion", "spirits of doubt", "spirits of complacency or despair", "spirits

---

[62] 2 Corinthians 2:7–11.

[63] 2 Corinthians 11:14.

[64] 1 Thessalonians 2:18.

[65] 2 Timothy 2:26.

[66] 2 Corinthians 12:7.

[67] Romans 16:20.

[68] James D.G. Dunn, *The Theology of Paul the Apostle*, T. & T. Clark, Edinburgh, 1998, pp. 62–70, 122–128.

[69] Robert Guelich, "Spiritual Warfare: Jesus, Paul and Peretti", *Pneuma*, Spring 1991, vol. 13:1, p. 45.

[70] Matthew 12:35.

of jealousy or strife or murder". Sins of the flesh, not the demonic, oppose the Spirit. And Jesus never attributes the rejection of His message and ministry to territorial spirits that impede the ministry, in either Nazareth or Jerusalem or any other region. Nor do any of the apostles.[71]

In certain circles, spiritual warfare has become a primary means of understanding Christian life and is considered the "key" to personal and corporate revival. Peter Wagner, for instance, says that Carlos Annacondia's book, *Listen to Me, Satan!* "may well be regarded by future historians as one of the most important, if not *the* most important book of the revival literature of the 1990s".[72] Early in the novel, *This Present Darkness*, Peretti's theology and worldview is certainly made explicit. Pastor Hank says, "That's what the Gospel is all about, fighting Satan .... Maybe I'll win, maybe I won't come out alive. But God didn't tell me I'd come out alive; He just told me to stay and fight Satan .... Satan does want this town. I can't let him have it."[73]

After a careful study of the Old Testament, the Gospels and the writings of the apostles, however, one is hard-pressed to maintain a Scriptural basis for such a pervasive emphasis on spiritual warfare. Just as "demon possession" exaggerates the influence and control the demonic may have over a person, so the whole construct of spiritual warfare overstates the spiritual environment in which we live. Even in Ephesians 6:10–18, the "armour of God" passage that will receive detailed consideration in a subsequent chapter, we do not wage war, nor are we called to warfare. We merely *wrestle*.

---

[71] Interestingly, Paul felt that the Holy Spirit prevented him from preaching in Asia, and that the Spirit of Jesus would not allow Paul and Barnabas to enter Bithynia (Acts 16:6–7).

[72] Carlos Annacondia, *Listen to Me, Satan!*, Creation House, 1998, p. vii (emphasis in the original).

[73] *Darkness*, p. 70.

In the opening chapter of Luke's Gospel, Zechariah is given the gift of silence for the duration of his wife Elizabeth's pregnancy. He is duly humbled and when his speech is restored, he praises the Lord's sovereign authority. Unfortunately, the NIV doesn't reflect the redemptive symmetry, for Zechariah holds warfare and worship in dynamic tension.[74]

> "Praise to the Lord, the God of Israel! For He has turned to His people and set them free. He has raised for us a strong deliverer ... So He promised: age after age He proclaimed by the lips of His holy prophets, that He would deliver us from our enemies ... [and] rescue us from enemy hands and set us free from fear, so that we might worship in His presence in holiness and righteousness our whole life long."

Zechariah finishes his song of praise with a prophetic picture that mirrors the opening verses of Genesis 1 and speaks yet again of the re-creative and restorative grace that will be made manifest with the coming of the Messiah: "In the tender compassion of our God the dawn from heaven will break upon us, to shine on those who live in darkness, under the shadow of death, and to guide our feet into the way of peace."[75]

This passage may well be the most succinct and carefully nuanced delineation of spiritual warfare anywhere in the Scriptures: the Lord delivers us from our enemies and sets us free from fear, and guides our feet into the way of peace that we might worship in holiness and righteousness. This call to worship is the re-sounding of Jehoshaphat's military strategy and as such, has timeless consequence:

> "Do not fear or be dismayed by this great horde, for the battle is in God's hands, not yours. Go down and engage them tomorrow ... it is not you who fight this battle; stand firm and wait, and

[74] Luke 1:68–74.
[75] Luke 1:78.

you will see the deliverance worked by the Lord for you . . . .
Praise the splendour of the Lord's holiness . . . . March out before
the troops, singing.''[76]

As the battle is in the God's hands, the Scriptures give clear
and repeated mandates to *"magnify the Lord"*.[77] When the
adversary comes against us, he is never the one to draw our
attention. Instead, we *"magnify the Lord"*. As with a magnifying
glass, we intensify our focus on Jesus, and "make Him
big" – bigger than any attack of the enemy, bigger than any
fear, bigger than any work of darkness, rejoicing in the
knowledge that *"He delivers us from our enemies . . . and rescues
us from enemy hands"*.

---

[76]   2 Chronicles 20:15–21.
[77]   Psalms 34:3; 35:27; 40:16; 69:30; 70:4; Luke 1:46, NASB.

Chapter 6

Shadow Realities

"I can see clearly now, the rain has gone.
I can see all obstacles in my way.
Gone are the dark clouds that had me blind;
It's gonna be a bright, sun-shiny day."
(Johnny Nash – 1972)

We know the speed of light – it was deduced by the Danish astronomer Olaf Roemer, who, in 1676, was studying mathematical anomalies in Jupiter's lunar eclipses. His estimate of 186,000 miles per second was remarkably accurate.

No one, to date, has ever measured the speed of dark.

It isn't because it's hard to do; it's that it's impossible. Alternative physics is of no help either – that, because darkness *de facto* does not exist. The dictionary definition of darkness as simply, "The absence of light".

If it were possible, for instance, to completely black-out a large sanctuary, those afraid of the dark would be most unsettled if they found themselves alone in there. The "blackness" might seem huge, even overwhelming. Everything would change, however, if even a single candle were lit and placed in the middle of that large black space. As proportionally small as the candle is, it overwhelms the darkness and penetrates into the furthest corners of the room.

Though darkness is only the absence of light, we nevertheless "see" it in the physical realm; so also we "see" the

83

works of darkness in the spiritual realm. But spiritual darkness is also an absence of light. The reality of evil and the forces of darkness cannot be denied. They put Jesus to death. The truth of their essence, however, is a compelling recognition that they are but an inferior reality, for three days later, God raised Jesus from the dead.

This is a concept that may still be elusive. A shadow is real, but it is an inferior reality. A shadow only exists because of a greater reality, the presence of a brightly shining light.

The forces of evil are "shadow" realities.

Though the darkness about us has filled human history with its horrors, it is an inferior reality that is dispelled by even a tiny revelation of ultimate reality. In his prologue, the apostle John says of Jesus, *"In Him was life, and that life was the light of mankind."* [1] John then makes two categorical declarations: *"The light shines in the darkness"* and *"the darkness has never overcome it"*. [2] The Greek verb *katalambanein* is a challenge to interpret, so some translations render it *"understood"*, rather than *"overcome"*, but as John presents his Gospel, darkness is not something which seeks to understand light, if that were possible. Rather, darkness is a spiritual force – one that is contrary and inferior to the light.

Midway through John's Gospel, Jesus says, *"I am the light of the world. No follower of mine shall walk in darkness; he shall have the light of life."* [3] Both here and in the prologue there are clearly intended parallels to the creation story; in Jesus, the darkness is even more completely bound; the chaos is even more completely restored to order; the desolation even more completely redeemed.

---

[1] John 1:4.

[2] John 1:5, NRSV.

[3] John 8:12.

There is no way of knowing whether or not Paul was familiar with the Lord's teaching in what we know as the Sermon on the Mount. There is certainly a very close similarity between Lord's words to His followers, *"You are the light for all the world"*[4] and the apostle's instruction in Ephesians, *"once you were darkness, now as Christians* [literally, "in the Lord"], *you are light . . . and whatever is exposed to the light itself becomes light".*[5]

Neither declaration is empty rhetoric. In January 2003, I was in Genoa, Italy, at one of Betel's men's houses. It is a large twelve-room house in the mountains north of the city. At the time, it was one of Betel's most challenged communities. Since its founding, it had a four-year heartache of repeated leadership failure, community division and rebellion. The new guys left disproportionately distressed and the residents complained of frequent nightmares. The centre never grew beyond ten men.

As soon as I stepped on site, I felt creepy. That feeling intensified as my hosts took me on a welcome tour. Thereafter, we had supper and as it was late, we went straight to bed.

That night, I had another interactive nightmare. Out of nowhere, a huge, dark grey cat attacked me. It was so vivid I sat bolt upright and doing so, I whacked my head on the bunk above me. Nursing the goose egg on my scalp the next morning over breakfast, I asked if the house leader knew any of the local history. (This is not the sort of question I typically ask, for I am far more interested in the mysteries of God than I am in the intrigues of human history.) The house leader told me that this was called *Casa Negro*, the "Black House". It was Mussolini's headquarters during World War II. Many of the *Partigiani* – the Italian Resistance – were mercilessly tortured in the basement of the building.

At the devotional that followed our coffee and rolls, I taught about Legion's deliverance and his familiar spirits. I underlined that they were squatters – illegitimate residents. We then

[4] Matthew 5:14.
[5] Ephesians 5:8, 13.

turned to Matthew 10:12 and the apostolic commission: *"Wish the house peace as you enter it."* Implicit is a Kingdom peace that can be imparted, one that is greater than any turmoil. I then spoke about consecration and anointing.

Twelve of us paraded up four flights of stairs, ducked under the low roof of the attic and scrambled onto the tower. It was not only the highest place on the property; the previous house leader had chosen it as the location for a most inglorious fall. He had gone out and scored a large quantity of heroin. It was bad enough that he was going to return to his hell; what made things worse was that he hosted a shooting party for the residents. Together, the whole house of men got high.

In the name of Jesus we commanded all unclean spirits to depart and give place to the Holy Spirit. We consecrated a large bowl of olive oil, poured portions of it into cereal bowls and sent the guys out to anoint anything that seemed unclean. They oiled everything in sight all the while speaking God's peace.

Two months later I received an email from the director of Betel Italy, Lindsay McKenzie. The community in Genoa had suddenly grown to over thirty men and was now the strongest and healthiest Betel in Italy. The new guys no longer seemed distressed. Community conflict was described as "normal".

Lindsay concluded with this last update: one of the guys had painted a sign that now hung outside on the wall. They had renamed the place *Casa Luce*, the "House of Light". The new name is a wonderful testimony to the transformative revelation of ultimate reality dispelling the inferior – *"whatever is exposed to the light itself becomes light"*.[6]

In the apostle Paul's day, the seaport of Ephesus was the capital city of the Roman Province of Asia. The populace was held sway by the cult of Artemis, the goddess of fertility and banking

---

[6] Ephesians 5:8, 13.

and protector of debts, *"worshipped by all Asia and the civilized world"*.[7] The ruins of her temple are still considered one of the seven wonders of the ancient world. Luke records that under Paul's ministry, there were many *"extraordinary miracles"* and many were delivered from evil spirits. The new believers purged themselves of demonic influence by corporately burning their sorcery books, worth well over ten million dollars in today's currency.[8] To say that the local spiritual establishment felt threatened is an understatement.[9]

In his letter to the church in Ephesus, Paul makes no explicit reference to Artemis or any other of the resident powers of darkness whatsoever. He shows no interest in identifying the demonic powers or strongholds that influence the city. There is, however, the categorical declaration that *"Christ* [has been raised] *from the dead, and enthroned . . . in the heavenly realms, far above all government and authority, all power and dominion, and any title of sovereignty that commands allegiance, not only in this age but also in the age to come"*.[10] There is no scriptural record of any rebuke or any binding of the "strongholds" in Ephesus, or any other place. Whoever they are, whatever their mandate, whatever their origin, they are inferior realities and are subject to the absolute sovereign authority of the Lord Jesus Christ.

The language of power pervades the whole of the New Testament. Repeated reference is made to "thrones", "rulers", "kings", "dominions", "authorities", "cosmic powers", "spiritual forces" and "principalities and powers". After his detailed study of all of these phrases, Walter Wink concludes that this vocabulary is "imprecise, liquid, interchangeable and unsystematic".[11] Matthew, for instance, uses *archon* of a Jewish

[7] Acts 19:27.

[8] Acts 19:19; 50,000 drachmas = 136 years' worth of salary.

[9] Acts 19:23–34.

[10] Ephesians 1:20–21.

[11] Walter Wink, *Naming the Powers: the Language of Power in the New Testament*, Fortress Press, 1984, p. 7.

ruler,[12] and sixteen verses later the same word is used in
the context of *"the prince* [archon] *of demons"*.[13] John does the
same: Satan is named the *"prince"* of this world, but ten
verses later, the same Greek word is used of the Jewish
"authorities".[14]

While the different words are used very fluidly, what is
clear is that all powers, whether they are heavenly or earthly,
divine or human, spiritual or physical, invisible or structural,
have all been made subject to Christ.[15] Neither Jesus nor Paul
give any detailed information about the powers and their
influence on individuals and world events; both Jesus and Paul
left no room for any doubt as to the inferior nature of their
reality.

There is only one deliverance account in John's Gospel for
instance. Jesus says, *"Now is the hour of judgment for this world;
now shall the prince of this world be driven out."*[16] In his hymn of
praise to Christ, Paul says *"In him everything in heaven and on
earth was created, not only things visible but also the invisible orders
of thrones, sovereignties, authorities, and powers: the whole universe
has been created through him and for him."*[17] Similarly, Paul
concludes his great Romans 8 Spirit theology with a rhetorical
question: *"what can separate us from the love of Christ?"* Wink
states, "The rest of the paragraph is a rising crescendo of
phrases that thunder louder and louder, No one! No one! No
one at all!"[18] The apostle bursts into doxology:

> *"I am convinced that there is nothing in death or life, in the
> realm of spirits or superhuman powers, in the world as it is or
> the world as it shall be, in the forces of the universe, in heights*

[12]   Matthew 9:18.
[13]   Matthew 9:34.
[14]   John 12:31, 42.
[15]   Walter Wink, *Naming the Powers*, p. 11.
[16]   John 12:31.
[17]   Colossians 1:16.
[18]   Walter Wink, *Naming the Powers*, p. 48.

or depths – nothing in all creation that can separate us from the love of God in Christ Jesus our Lord."[19]

That conviction is the ground of victory, won in faith. We surrender that ground when we treat the demonic and the powers of darkness as anything more than inferior reality. Heinrich Schlier, in his careful study, *Principalities and Powers in the New Testament*, makes the bold and compelling assertion: "Christ has left the devil only whatever power unbelief allows him."[20]

An overemphasis on the demonic and warfare is not a new problem. More than sixteen hundred years ago, Chrysostom addressed the issues at length, especially in a sermon titled, "Against Those Who Say that Demons Govern Human Affairs". He begins at the beginning, with a consideration of the fall. Chrysostom traces the grave consequences of Adam and Eve's disobedience and concludes that there is something at work in each of us that "wastes what has been given". He then quickly changes focus, from the "inferior" reality of fallen creation, to a gloriously redemptive perspective. He says that in the grace of God, "we received afterwards gifts greater than those lost. In place of temporal toil He honoured us with eternal life. In place of thorns and thistles He prepared the fruit of the Spirit to grow in our souls . . . . God made the gain greater than the loss."[21]

Page after page, Chrysostom tries to redress the excessive attention that was being given to the evil one and his inferior realities. "Some dare to say that demons administer our affairs. What can I do? You have a loving Master. He chooses rather to be blasphemed by you through these words, than to commit

[19] Romans 8:38–39.

[20] *Principalities and Powers in the New Testament*, New York, Herder and Herder, 1961, p. 58.

[21] *Nicene and Ante-Nicene Fathers*, First Series, vol. 9, Hendrickson Pub., Peabody, Mass., 1994, p. 179.

your affairs to the demons and thus persuade you by the reality how demons administer."[22] Chrysostom's focus is riveted on ultimate reality, as reflected in his comments on Legion's deliverance: "[The demons] would have done to the possessed the things which they did to the swine, had not the demoniacs in their very madness experienced the providence of God. Now therefore when you see a man excited by a demon, worship the Master."[23]

Characteristically, the New Testament imagery and context for all this power language is far more political than military: authorities, powers, dominions, thrones – not armies, battles, or forces. The apostle John never uses any military language whatsoever, but does make the summary statement that, *"the Son of God appeared for the very purpose of undoing the devil's work".*[24]

Paul certainly speaks more of a power struggle than a war and when he does use a warfare metaphor, it is pitched in the past tense. "[On the cross, Christ] *disarmed the cosmic powers and authorities and made a public spectacle of them, leading them as captives in His triumphal procession."*[25] The syntax presumes a conflict that has already been conducted and concluded. Commenting on this passage, Chrysostom stated, "There was, as it were, a single combat. Death wounded Christ: but Christ, being wounded, did afterwards kill death."[26]

While conducting my research for this book, I stumbled across a five-page work titled *The Descent of Christ into Hell.* It was probably written towards the end of the third century and though it reads almost playfully, it was nevertheless written to

[22] *Ibid.*, p. 183.
[23] *Ibid.*
[24] 1 John 3:8.
[25] Colossians 2:15.
[26] Homily VI, Colossians, Nicene and Post-Nicene Fathers, vol. 13, Hendrickson Pub., Peabody, Mass., p. 287.

convey a great deal of theology. It certainly brings telling insights into how the Church understood the character and mission of the devil; more importantly, it graphically describes the cosmic dynamics of the redemption Christ accomplished through His death on the cross. It, too, reads as a single demonstration of the Lord's power rather than a protracted war.

By way of literary genre, it reads like a cross between an abbreviated *Paradise Lost* and *The Screwtape Letters*. The balance of the narrative takes place in hell, between Satan and Hades, personified, just before Jesus was handed over to be crucified. Satan's syntax is all inverted – his "good" is only good in an inferior reality, as is made abundantly clear as he tells Hades of Jesus:

> "Satan, the heir of darkness said to Hades, 'O all-devouring and insatiable, hear of Jesus . . . He has done me many evils when living with mortals in the upper world. For wherever He found my servants, He persecuted them; and whatever men I made crooked, blind, lame, lepers, or any such thing, by a single word He healed them; and many whom I had got ready to be buried, even these through a single word He brought to life again.' "

Hades knew none of this and so asks in ignorance, "Is this man so powerful as to do such things by a single word? Or if He be so, how can you possibly withstand Him?"

Satan responds cockily, "O all-devouring and insatiable Hades, are you so afraid at hearing of our common enemy? Make ready, in order that you may lay fast hold of Him when He comes."

Hades isn't so sure any of this is a good idea.

> "Heir of darkness, son of destruction, devil . . . not long ago I swallowed down one dead, Lazarus by name; and

not long after, one of the living by a single word dragged him up by force out of my bowels: and I think that it was He of whom you speak. If, therefore we receive Him here, I am afraid that perchance we be in danger even about the rest .... Wherefore I adjure you, for your benefit and mine, do not bring Him here; for I think that He is coming here to raise all the dead. And this I tell you: by the darkness in which we live, if you bring Him here, not one of the dead will be left behind."

While they're arguing back and forth, a great voice like thunder sounds, "Lift up your gates O you rulers; and be lifted up you everlasting doors; and the King of Glory shall come in."²⁷ Hades and Satan rally their troops and try to batten down the hatches. Heaven continues to thunder and Hades asks fearfully, "Who is the King of Glory?"

The angels of the Lord sing out, *The LORD strong and mighty, the LORD mighty in battle.*"²⁸ With those words, the brazen gates of hell are shattered. The iron bars are broken, those long bound come out of their prisons, "and the King of Glory came in ... and all the dark places of Hades were lighted up".

Hades cries out, "Who comes here without sin, one who is seen to be so small and yet of such great power, so lowly yet exalted...?"

Jesus doesn't answer the question directly. Instead, "The King of Glory seized Satan by the head and delivered him to his angels, and said, 'With iron chains bind his hands, and his feet, and his neck, and his mouth.'" Then He delivers him to Hades and says, "Take him, and keep him secure till my second coming."

Hades then has a thing or two to say to Satan. Roughly translated, it goes something like "WHAT were you thinking?"

---

²⁷ Psalm 24:7.

²⁸ Psalm 24:8.

"Beelzebub, heir of fire and punishment, enemy of the saints, why did you bring about the King of Glory's crucifixion, such that He should come here and deprive us of our power? Turn and see that not one of the dead has been left in me, but all that you gained through the tree of knowledge, you lost through the tree of the cross: and all your joy has been turned into grief; and wishing to put to death the King of Glory, you have put yourself to death . . . . O arch-devil, the beginning of death, root of sin, end of all evil, what evil did you find in Jesus, that you should compass His destruction? [Why did you] bring such a man into this darkness, through whom you have been deprived of all who have died . . . ?"[29]

Christ's victory over the evil one is so commanding it reaches to the depths of hell.[30] It also extends to us as believers, and beyond, to the heavenly realms. In Ephesians 2:4 Paul says, *"because of [God's] great love for us, he brought us to life with Christ when we were dead because of our sins."* Though our own personal lusts and wickedness were the source of our sin, there was also more going on. Paul says, *"you formerly walked according to the course of this world, according to the prince of the power of the air, of the spirit that is now working in the sons of disobedience."*[31]

God's mercy is so comprehensive that we have not only been saved from our sins and delivered from the spiritual rule of the evil one; we have also been *"raised . . . up in union with Christ Jesus and enthroned . . . with Him in the heavenly realms, so*

---

[29] *The Descent of Christ into Hell*, Ante-Nicene Fathers, vol. 8, Hendrickson Pub., Peabody, Mass., 1994, pp. 436–7.

[30] 1 Peter 3:19; 4:6.

[31] Ephesians 2:2, NASB. The NIV inappropriately translates the key phrase as "ruler of the kingdom of the air", but the Greek word for kingdom, *basileia*, is not used in this passage. *Exousias* is to be translated "power" as found also in the NKJV and NRSV, *"prince of the power of the air"*.

that He might display in the ages to come how immense are the resources of His grace, and how great His kindnesses to us in Christ Jesus".[32]

Our position in Christ is somehow an ongoing testimony in the heavenly realms, for it seems that our peace, our freedom and our graced lives further torment the powers and principalities. When we put a smile on our faces, fill our mouths with praise and let the light in our eyes shine, we demonstrate to the powers of the air that we are, with Christ, *"more than conquerors".*[33]

Conversely, if we dump and grump and act like Eeyore: "Good morning, if it is, which I doubt..." we are choosing to live under an inferior reality, living as losers rather than victors. Satan is already cast down and as Chrysostom put it, "Already then am I conqueror, for he [the devil] is already cast down and in a state of ruin; and his victory consists not in being himself crowned, but in effecting [our] ruin."[34]

For us in Christ, focus is everything. Our "warfare" is conducted by shifting our attention from our present circumstances to the finished work of Christ and all that is ours in Him. His finish is where we begin.

Over and against the inferior reality of the darkness round about us, we are invited to live in the revelation of what truly *is*, in Christ.

Perhaps we do know the speed of dark. In AD 385, Gregory of Nyssa, one of the church fathers from central Turkey described the Gospel mystery as "Power conjoined with Love." In his *Great Catechism* he states, "It is the particular effect of light to make darkness vanish and of life to destroy death ...."

[32] Ephesians 2:6–7.

[33] Romans 8:37, NIV.

[34] *Nicene and Post-Nicene Fathers*, First Series, vol. 13, Hendrickson Pub., Peabody, Mass., 1994, p. 162.

It is not in the nature of darkness to remain when light is present or of death to exist when life is active." [35]

That would mean that the speed of dark is 186,000 miles per second – as it is driven back by the light!

[35] Gregory of Nyssa, Nicene and Post-Nicene Fathers, Second Series, vol. 5, Hendrickson Pub., Peabody, Mass., 1994, p. 494.

Chapter 7

Lies, All Lies

*"All warfare is based on deception. An indispensable preliminary
to battle is to attack the mind of the enemy."*
(Sun Tzu, *The Art of War*)[1]

✧ ✧ ✧

Each and every one of us lives somewhere on a continuum of influence. The likes of Legion and St. Francis of Assisi would be found on the opposite and extreme ends. Just as Legion – the most tormented human in all the Gospels – was profoundly influenced and crazed by demonic spirits, so Francis – one of the most Christlike humans that has ever lived – was gloriously influenced and blessed by the Spirit of God. We all find ourselves somewhere between those two extremes.

A believer is, or at least should be, someone who is "under the influence" of the Holy Spirit. There should be ongoing, wilful surrender to the influence of His leading, guiding and transformative presence. But there would be very few of us who have never experienced a meltdown whereby we completely lost the plot for a while. In moments of extreme desperation I've certainly vented disproportionate frustration and anger, such that in its wake, there is only one appropriate response: "Call the exorcist. Where did *that* come from?"

But a flippant, "The devil made me do it" attitude glosses over critical dynamics. I must always take personal responsibility

[1] *The Art of War*, Sun Tzu, trans. Samuel Griffith, Oxford, 1963, pp. 41, 66.

for the ways in which I express my anger. It is also mine to ask forgiveness and make peace with those whom I've hurt and wronged. However, consideration needs to be given to those times when either tangibly or insidiously, it feels as though "something came over me".

Some marker posts need to be established on the continuum of influence before proceeding. Not all unbelievers are demonized. Both believers and unbelievers contend with "carnal desires". If these desires are nurtured and indulged they take on the power of sin. If the sin is habituated, demonic influence takes root, and if perpetuated, the habit becomes a lifestyle. Conversely, if carnal desires are disciplined and a fresh filling of the Holy Spirit is received, His influence grows into an ever-deepening holiness and freedom.

Inevitably, the question is raised, "Can believers have a demon?" The answer is, "Yes, but why would they want one? They're not pets."

A believer can be demonized in one of two ways. If they were demonized before their conversion and they have not been discipled, it is possible for a part of their lives to be so un-surrendered to the Lordship of Christ that demonic influence still holds an oppressive sway. The early Church attended to this very issue by requiring thorough instruction and ministry prior to baptism. For instance, Cyril of Jerusalem proposed a two-year period of preparation and as part of the baptismal service, a candidate was asked, "Do you renounce Satan and all his works, all his pomp and all his service?"[2] After a three-fold renunciation, the candidate was then blessed with the prayer, "In the name of Jesus Christ I command all unclean spirits to depart and give place to the Holy Spirit."

The second way a believer can be demonized is through

[2] Cyril of Jerusalem, "Lecture XIX, First Lecture on the Mysteries", Catechetical Lectures, Nicene and Post Nicene Fathers, Second Series, vol. 7, Hendrickson Pub., Peabody, Mass., 1994, pp. 144–146.

wilful disobedience or rebellion. Chrysostom preached extensively on temptations, deliverance and overcoming the demonic. He addressed this very issue:

> "How then, you may ask, are we to wrestle with the darkness?"
> "By becoming light."
> "How do we wrestle against the 'spiritual hosts of wickedness?'"
> "By becoming good."
> "For wickedness is contrary to good, and light drives away darkness. If we ourselves too be darkness, we shall inevitably be taken captive. How then shall we overcome? If, what they [the demons] are by nature, that we become by choice, we are surely to be vanquished."[3]

Most of us, most of the time, live in the middle of the continuum. It is where most of us wrestle, most of the time. The good news is that there are very, very few Legions.

In Ephesians 6:11 Paul writes that we are to *"stand firm against the stratagems of the devil"*. The Greek word translated "stratagems" or "schemes" is *methodeia*. Its verb cousin, *methodeuo*, means "to defraud". Satan's essential character and method is to deceive, to lie and to steal, but he is not very imaginative. He has three basic methods and it is against these three strategies that most of us wrestle, most of the time.

In this regard, a little book titled *The Art of War* is most instructive. It may well be the earliest essay on war ever written, probably composed during the fourth century BC. One translator has said that it stands as the "concentrated essence of wisdom on the conduct of war and has never been surpassed in

---

[3] John Chrysostom, "Homilies on Ephesians", XXII, Nicene and Post-Nicene Fathers, First Series, vol. 13, Hendrickson Pub., Peabody, Mass., p. 161.

comprehension and depth of understanding."[4] Though the warfare Sun Tzu writes about is military in nature, many of his principles bring remarkable insights to bear on spiritual conflicts. The quote that heads this chapter is but one example: "All warfare is based on deception. An indispensable preliminary to battle is to attack the mind of the enemy."[5]

This is precisely how our enemy works against us: he is continuously attempting to deceive us and attack our minds. The devil's first ploy was to dishonour the character of God and it is that which he ever hopes to perpetuate. In the Garden of Eden, the devil manifests as the serpent and asks Eve, *"Is it true . . . ?"* Those three words shake creation to its very foundations and eternity hangs in the balance. "Is what God said true?"

In answer to the question, Eve repeats what she has been told. *"God has forbidden us to eat the fruit of the tree* [in the middle of the garden] *. . . if we do, we shall die."*[6] With compelling assurance the serpent responds, *"Of course you will not die."* The sly one promotes himself as the truth-teller and subtly implies that God is the one who misleads. This is ever the deceiver's method of attack: he attempts to erode our faith in the faithfulness of God.

Though he wrote nearly eighteen hundred years ago, there is a timelessness to the comments that Origen brings to bear in his treatise *On the Opposing Powers*:

> [The demons drive us] to excess of anger or sorrow, or to the last pitch of despair, or when fatigued and overcome by any annoyances, to make complaints against God, as One who does not administer human life justly and equitably; the consequence of which is that our faith may be weakened, or our hopes disappointed, or we may be

4 *The Art of War*, p. v.
5 *The Art of War*, pp. 41, 66.
6 Genesis 3:3.

compelled to give up the truth of our faith, or be led to entertain irreligious sentiments regarding God."[7]

If honest, most of us would be quick to affirm, "Been there, done that."

"Why is there victory for everyone but me?"

"Why do God's promises come true for everyone else?"

"I can't read promises of the Lord's tender care and unfailing love – what a joke."

"God doesn't love me, He doesn't care what I'm going through; He's deaf to my prayers . . . ."

The stratagems of the evil one are such that we will be tempted in all sorts of ways to believe that the Kingdom has not come near, at least to us. Lying voices try to convince us that we're still strangers to God's love, grace and mercy, that we must still be bound in our sins, that we are still under condemnation, that we are still unworthy.

Sun Tzu was right: "All warfare is based on deception." Our enemy is ever whispering lies about God, lies about our souls and lies about our spirits, our minds and our self-images. We're lied to about what's most important in life and lied to about what we really need. We're lied to about our past and our futures. We're lied to personally, corporately and socially.

Our enemy uses a second strategy against us, one that is also based on deception. It merely has a different focus. Regrettably, it's not an either/or attack, but rather, a both/and. While the devil is attempting to cause us to find fault with the nature and character of our Heavenly Father, he is also ever drawing us to find fault with one another. It is the essence of the distorted promise he makes to Eve: *"you will be like God himself, knowing both good and evil."*[8] This deception is the telling of two half-truths. One is an understatement, the other an exaggeration.

[7] Origen, *On the Opposing Powers*, Ante-Nicene Fathers, vol. 4, Hendrickson Pub., Peabody, Mass., p. 333.

[8] Genesis 3:5.

Firstly, the serpent lied, for we are not *like God*; we are made *"in His image"*.[9] Secondly, while we know both good and evil, it is an imperfect knowledge, something considerably short of God's full understanding. This partial knowledge is the source of the fault-finding and judgmentalism that tears at our relationships. Interestingly, the origins of the Greek word *daimon* – "demon" – means, "to disrupt, to rend and tear".[10]

The enemy attacks our minds and seeks to rend our relationships through faultfinding, often with and by those closest and dearest to us. Our spiritual forebears were victimized by this very strategy. Before the Fall, Adam and Eve enjoyed perfect freedom with one another and presumably took complete delight in one another's nakedness. But once *"the eyes of both of them were opened"*[11] they could no longer be so vulnerable to one another.

Perhaps it went something like this. Adam looked down at himself and then looked at Eve. He looked down at himself and looked at Eve again. Then he said, "Eve, what's wrong with you? Why don't you have one of these?" She looked at Adam, looked at herself, looked at Adam and said, "I don't know, but I'd rather have two of these than one of those silly looking things." And with those accusations, they wounded each other so profoundly that they had to hide themselves from one another.

The third deceptive strategy comes against us as the consequence of the second. After Adam and Eve found fault with one another, they tried to hide, not just from one another, but also from God. When the Lord comes calling, Adam defensively answers, *"I was afraid because I was naked, so I hid."*[12] The enemy's influence profoundly distorted Adam's self-understanding so that a sense of fear and shame pervaded. In

---

[9] Genesis 1:27.
[10] Werner Foerster, *Theological Dictionary of the New Testament*, vol. II, Eerdmans, Grand Rapids, 1964, p. 2.
[11] Genesis 3:7.
[12] Genesis 3:10.

this, Belial, the "unworthy one," ever attempts to impart feelings of unworthiness to his victims.

Just as we each find something of our "original" self in the account of Adam and Eve's creation, temptation and fall, so we also find something of our deepest self in the parable of the prodigal son. When he finally comes to his senses and heads for home, his confession is an admixture of both truth and distortion: *"Father, I have sinned against heaven and against you. I am no longer worthy to be called your son."*[13]

The lie is pre-empted by his dad's unconditional love and unfailing mercy: *"Quick! Fetch a robe, the best we have, and put it on him; put a ring on his finger and sandals on his feet. Bring the fatted calf and kill it, and let us celebrate with a feast. For this son of mine was dead and has come back to life; he was lost and is found."*[14] Because Father's love so completely restores all that sin destroys, the feelings of unworthiness have no place or grounding.

The dynamics of the Lord's High Priestly prayer can appropriately be applied at this very point, not only for the prodigal, but to the prodigal in each of us: *"I do not pray you to take them out of the world, but to keep them from the evil one ... Consecrate them by the truth; your word is truth."*[15] It is but one aspect of divine mystery that Adam and Eve's eyes were "opened" when they succumbed to deception, yet it is a revelation of truth that redeems, restores and sets us free.

Another piece of mystery is the place the evil one's schemings have in the providence of God. If one can tolerate the irreverence, it's helpful to cast the Lord's admonitions to Peter in a good news/bad news format. Jesus says,

---

[13] Luke 15:21, NIV.
[14] Luke 15:22–24.
[15] John 17:15.

"I have good news for you Peter – you are the Rock and on this rock I will build My Church; I give to you the keys of the Kingdom and the gates of hell shall not prevail.

"The bad news is, Satan's asked permission to sift you like wheat.

"The good news is, he had to ask permission.

"The bad news is, I gave it to him.

"The good news is, I'm praying for you.

"The bad news is, you need it.

"The good news is, your inheritance is reserved in Heaven and nothing can destroy or spoil it.

"The bad news is, you're going to deny Me three times.

"The good news is, after this is all over you'll be stronger and you'll give strength to your brothers." [16]

The Lord's prayers turn Peter's impetuous instability and uncertain character into responsible leadership and ultimately establish in him a faith strong enough to endure martyrdom. Jesus as our intercessor is even now praying that we find our strength in Him and all that He has accomplished. [17]

In the Greek, Jesus prays that Peter's faith may not fail, *eklipae*, that Peter's faith may not be *eclipsed*. This word study came by way of revelation, for I immediately thought of the scene in the movie *Apollo 13* when Tom Hanks looks up at the full moon, closes one eye, points his arm to the heavens and eclipses the moon with his thumbnail.

Even if one has a skinny thumb, that square one inch is enough to obscure 75 million square kilometres of the moon's visible surface. Jesus is praying that the infinitesimally smaller not eclipse the greater, because of perspective. This distortion I know all too well, for there are certainly times in my life when troubling circumstances eclipse the greater revelation of what I do know of God's love and faithfulness.

[16] Matthew 16:18–19; Luke 22:31–32; 1 Peter 1:4.
[17] Romans 8:34; Hebrews 7:25.

So often I don't understand why tragedy, misfortune and disaster befall us – why the disappointments, the failures, the delays. They seem so big, so overwhelming. But I hope that I'm way beyond the temptation to give up and let go of what I do understand, what I have known of my Heavenly Father's *"unfailing love* [that] *reaches to the heavens,* [His] *faithfulness to the skies"*.[18] To do so would be to give up and settle for so much less than I had before the disappointment.

I take further comfort in the knowledge that Satan had to ask permission to do his sifting, just as he had to receive permission before he could have a go at Job.[19] And just as with the testing of this Old Testament hero, God very deliberately sets the boundaries and limits of the assaults – "Thus far and no further." Nevertheless, in both of the trials, Satan is basically told, "Have at him." In Peter's case, it is sobering to realize that Jesus is fully aware of Satan's planned torment, yet He doesn't bind it, or rebuke it.

Only such a reminder keeps present demonic strategy from eclipsing the truth that the apostle Paul declares: *"All things work together for good to those who love God, to those who are called according to His purpose."*[20] I am coming to a place where I can rest in the knowledge that as with Peter, the Lord continues to be committed to a greater end, for the greater good of a greater number. As I face unchanging circumstances that seemingly elude breakthrough, I understand that it is not because the enemy has such great power, or holds tormenting control over my life. Rather, it is because God is allowing the sifting to build into me patient endurance and long-suffering. I only wish that the character grace of long-suffering could be forged within me more quickly.

I also understand that endurance is not living with gritted teeth. Rather, it's about waging patience as warfare. Any

---

[18]   Psalm 36:5.

[19]   Job 1:9–12; 2:5–6.

[20]   Romans 8:28, NKJV.

demonstration of the fruit of the Spirit is the antithesis of the demonic. If every time we're attacked and tempted to find fault, either with God or those around us, or when the accuser tries to stir up the feelings of worthlessness, we choose to worship and demonstrate more love, or joy, or gentleness, then we're becoming more like Christ and completely thwarting the enemy's attempts to destroy us.

Nearly a hundred years ago, John G. Lake commented on 1 John 4:4 in a sermon titled, "Spiritual Dominion".

> "If we had faith to believe that *greater is He that is in us*, bless God, we would be stepping out with boldness and majesty. The conscious supremacy of the Son of God would be manifest in our lives, and instead of being subservient and bowed down and broken beneath the weight of sin and the powers of darkness around us, THEY would flee from us and keep out of our way. I believe before God there is not a devil that comes within a hundred feet of a real God-anointed Christian."[21]

If we respond to the adversary's schemes in a spirit of worship and receive the sufficient grace to manifest more of the fruit of the Spirit, it becomes counterproductive for our enemy to attack, for it just makes us more like Jesus! It is for this very reason that our response to the evil one's strategies is a warfare of opposites. As he continues to deceive, we fight that deception with truth.

Just as I was finishing this chapter, one of my host pastors told me of what he had faced over the last few months. Paul Lynch is the senior leader of King's Church in Amersham, England. He

---

[21] *John G. Lake: His Life, His Sermons, His Boldness of Faith*, Kenneth Copeland Pubs., Fort Worth, 1994, pp. 145–6. Emphasis in the original.

and his wife Liz had planned a missions trip in early April to Ghana, West Africa, to visit some of the churches they support. They needed several inoculations and on 7th February he had his yellow fever jab. The nurse told him that there was a slight possibility of a reaction. If it occurred, it would happen within five to ten days. It would be mild – he might experience headaches, fever, joint aches and pains, but it would last only twenty-four hours.

On the 12th of February, a headache set in, as did the joint pain and fever. The next day he felt worse. He was in bed the following four days and as he and Liz were concerned that this was lasting longer than they were told it would, he dragged himself to the doctor's. Blood tests revealed a high enzyme count, signalling an acute attack on his liver. Six days later the tests were repeated and though Paul had started to feel a bit better, the results showed no improvement in the high enzyme count.

Paul's doctor initially told him that sometimes it takes weeks if not months for the levels to return to normal, but that there was nothing to worry about – in time, his levels would return to normal.

In his gentle Scottish brogue, Paul said, "When I left the doctor's surgery, I had such a spiritual attack, unlike any I'd ever had before. A darkness, a cloud, descended and I started believing that things were going drastically wrong. I thought I was dying. I kept thinking about my thanksgiving service. My main concern was my family. We lost our seventeen-year-old daughter only four years previously and I didn't know how my wife, son and remaining daughter would cope with losing me as well. I wasn't afraid of dying; I was just so apprehensive thinking about how everybody would fare without me.

"On the return visit, my doctor, Bryn, said, 'There is no long-term damage and there are no signs of abuse to your liver,' but as soon as he said that, something else said, 'Yes there is. Your time's up. Get ready. You've done whatever you've come here to do. You're finished.'

"Those voices were so real, so strong, they were almost audible. It was like an invasion. I was constantly bombarded my every waking moment. I've never experienced such spiritual attack. I descended into emotional depths I've never been to before. Liz and I were out shopping, for instance, and she reminded me that I needed to get some rechargeable batteries for the camera. As I'm walking the aisles, thoughts flooded my mind: 'What do you need batteries for? You're never going to get to use your camera.' Our daughter is newly married and when she came to mind, I had thoughts like, 'You'll never get to see your grandchildren; you won't be here.'

"It wasn't until I was in the deepest, darkest pit I've ever been in that God clearly said to me two things: 'You've got to trust Me, because I am the truth; and you've got to trust those that I've brought into your life, because they speak the truth.'

"I had gone to the clinic for yet another blood test and Bryn called me with the results. He said that the levels still hadn't dropped, but he said, 'You need to hear me – you will be OK.' I left the clinic and went for a walk and it was then that the Lord spoke to me. Bryn is not only a great doctor; he's a good brother and he always speaks the truth. The Lord was telling me I had to trust him. I had to take hold of the truth, embrace the truth and live in the truth, and when I did this, something broke spiritually, emotionally, mentally and physically. The darkness dispelled and Liz said my whole countenance changed. My appetite returned and I started to sleep again that night. Virtually the next day, I felt so much stronger.

"The afternoon things broke, a man in the church passed me as I was leaving the doctor's office. He phoned that evening and said he felt that Satan was trying to take me out. The picture he saw was of a skittle and a bowling ball, and Satan was coming

right for me. God had told him that what I was suffering was
not physical sickness but a spiritual battle. He assured me of his
prayers.

"That same day, a lady in the church had a vision of a pack of
snarling wolves surrounding me and God told her that she had
to pray for me that I'd be steadfast.

"The following day I felt well enough to go to the Partners
in Harvest conference in Hemel Hempstead and that evening,
during a time of prayer ministry, Nev Green came up and
stood in front of me. He didn't say anything for quite a while
and then he shared the verse where Jesus said, 'Satan has asked
permission to sift you as wheat, but I am praying for you.'
Nev then said, 'You need to understand two things. One is,
Satan has had to ask Jesus and Jesus has allowed it, and second,
when that sifting is finished, you will come back like Peter,
in strength and in courage and of greater service to your
brothers.'

"In retrospect, there's a part of me that wishes I'd received all
of those words and encouragements before all of this happened,
so I could have been prepared, but I know that I've learned
more about myself and more about God during those dark days
than I would have if I knew what was going on.

"I know that I'll never be the same again. I wake up in the
morning and I'm just so grateful for another day. My first
thoughts are, 'God, I just want to seize this day for You.' There
had been a certain dullness over me, in me, for years. I felt like I
was on a treadmill of ritual and routine, just going through the
motions. Now finally I feel like I'm firing on all cylinders and
I'm raring to go! It feels like it was a wake-up call.

"I'm seeing my wife differently; I'm seeing the church
differently. I have a love for the church that I didn't have
before this experience and God has changed my whole heart so
much. I've gone from 'My time's up, I'm finished' to 'God, You
give me the very breath I breathe and I'm so excited about what
You've got planned for me.'

"Though it wasn't a particularly long time, those are ten days Liz and I will never forget."

Sun Tzu was right. All warfare *is* based on deception. The good news is that in the mercy of God, the intensity of the warfare never exceeds the sufficiency of grace.

Chapter 8

Field Tested

"Plug it in and see what happens."
(Mr. Nevard)[1]

Rarely is life as tidy as theology. I have a good friend who would be best described as a devout sceptic, because he has trouble bridging the gap between the vicissitudes of life and the assertions of faith. Bruce comes from a German Mennonite background and in the course of our discussions he is continuously asking, "Does it *schtem?*"

Schtem is a very usable word. Regardless of what it is we're talking about, Bruce is asking, "Does it hold together? At the end of the day, does it work? Do the pieces of the puzzle fit together?"

As the title of this chapter indicates, Bruce's question is applied to the theology that has been presented thus far. Does it *schtem?*

Stacey Brecard[2] is a medical missionary who has given her life to care for some of the poorest of the poor. For the last three years she has lived in a tent in Manica in central Mozambique, southeast Africa. From her base, she and her teams conduct

---

[1] Mr. Nevard was my grade 11 electronics teacher.

[2] Her name has been changed. Because of her missions involvements, Stacey needs to maintain a low profile.

bush clinics and evangelistic outreaches throughout much of the nation. She presently works with a team of ten and has established three clinics.

I first met Stacey in May 2002 at a small conference centre just inside the South African border near Nelspruit. My dear friends, Rolland and Heidi Baker, the directors of Iris Ministries, had invited me to be the speaker at their annual staff retreat. Stacey was one of their invited guests. Since our first meeting we have crossed paths several times, both in Africa and in Canada.

Stacey is one of those rare human beings whom you're truly privileged to meet. She has a gentle spirit, a quick smile, bright and embracing eyes and carries an uncommon authority. She always leaves me feeling that I not only want to be a better person; I'm left knowing, that by the grace of God, I can and will be.

Stacey was not always that kind of person.

Growing up, she had a violent and unmanageable temper. Though she's just a little too tall to be petite, she'd get into fights all the time. She was extremely disciplined and thought that a career in the army would be a good fit. Her anger management only got worse. She didn't know how to communicate her feelings, so when someone was barking in her face, she'd just start swinging. Over time, she got more and more out of control – which alarmed her because she was a control freak. It also alarmed her superiors, so for everyone's wellbeing, she was honourably discharged.

Stacey had become a Christian while in the services, but still had a long way to go. "I was fairly legalistic in my thinking and at that time moral government was a strong teaching in the church I was involved in. I sucked it up. I loved it. I loved the standards – it was either 'black or white'. Unfortunately, one of the leaders fell into an immoral relationship. This was the guy who was telling me how to live a moral life.

"I was totally disillusioned. I grabbed my stuff and hitchhiked up into the Californian mountains and camped for almost three years. I lived all by myself and just read my Bible. Bit by bit I began to get involved in a small community church. Bill Johnson was the pastor and I started going to Kris Vallotton's home group. He and his wife lived in a log cabin in the woods.

"I was pretty rough-cut in those days. I didn't bathe all winter because I was camping and it was freezing and I didn't want to get wet. I didn't wash my hair for months. I'd crawl out of the woods and come to this home group. I stunk and I was very confrontational. Kris would be trying to teach and I'd interrupt, saying, 'That's not right.' I would challenge everything. I didn't have a lot of social graces. I didn't even know how to take turns in a conversation. But he and his wife never tried to change me from the outside. They never said, 'Don't come if you don't take a bath.' They just accepted me and loved me, just as I was. And it was their love and acceptance that dramatically changed my life. I have no idea where I'd be today without it.

"I went from the mountains to YWAM – Youth With A Mission, at their main base in Hawaii.

"I was in counselling school and they were teaching me about the Father heart of God. I understood God as my Lord, as my Master and as my Creator, but I didn't get the fatherhood thing. For most of my childhood, my father was in prison for armed robbery. There was no 'life with dad'. I'm listening to this teaching and trying to get my head around it all.

"After class I went for a walk and ended up at a small church. They'd made it available for us to hang out there and pray. That afternoon I had it to myself. While I was sitting in one of the pews I felt the Lord calling me to repent for the bitterness I felt towards my father. That thought threw me into a rage. 'Why do I have to repent? I was the kid, I was the victim. He was the adult.'

"I got so angry at God, I lost it. I started punching out the stained glass windows in the church and once my hands hurt too much, I started kicking holes in the doors. I went outside and overturned some of the tombstones in the cemetery and when I had completely exhausted myself, I realized I had done a really bad thing. I had just vandalized a church.

"I thought, 'When they find out about this, they're going to throw me out of school.' I ran back to the YWAM base and began packing up my bags. I was going to leave some money for the damages and just run off.

"As I was leaving, another student was just returning from the church. She had seen the mess and when she saw all the blood down the front of my trousers she realized I'd had a blow out. She ran and told the staff.

"When they caught up with me, I was extremely agitated. My knuckles were busted up. I was cut up from the glass and I was in no mood for their rebukes. I said, 'I know I did something wrong – I'll pay for the damages – and don't worry, I'm leaving.' Their response was not critical or judgmental. They said, 'Please work through this. Don't run away.' They encouraged me to stay and address my anger issues.

"This shocked me. I wasn't expecting that response. I was very legalistic and used to army discipline, so I wasn't expecting kindness or understanding. I decided to stay.

"The next day the same guy was teaching the Father heart of God again. This time I got the basics. I repented for my bitterness towards my father and immediately something changed. There was just a break. I felt God's compassion and love and acceptance despite myself. I felt such a freedom. It seemed like I was finally free from the violence.

"A few days later, the guest teacher was the National Director from the YWAM base in Australia. His first name was Tom. During the break in-between his sessions, he came up behind me. Somebody had told him what I'd done a couple of days before and he wanted to pray for me. He put his hands on my shoulders.

"All I saw out of the corner of my eye was some big guy

coming up and laying his hands on me, so I turned around and hit him so hard I knocked him down. And then I realized what I had done. I had just decked the guest speaker in front of the class. Worse, I thought I was free from the violence and I wasn't. I felt hopeless and I was embarrassed, and it suddenly felt like nothing had changed.

"I took off running. All the while I was thinking, 'I am going to seriously hurt someone, I am so out of control.' I just wanted to give up.

"I had run as far as the ocean cliffs and as I was standing there I heard a Hawaiian voice, 'You just go jump.' The voice was so real, I turned around, but nobody was there. That startled me and I thought, 'This is the devil's torment.' But he had overplayed his hand. I ran all the way back to the classroom and said 'I'm so sorry.'

"Tom forgave me and while I was still crying he prayed for me. But I was still so upset, I wasn't listening to his prayer. I felt something change though. The anger, the rage, the shame, was gone. Something had broken. I was told later that he prayed specifically against a spirit of violence and a spirit of anger.

"I have never had a violent episode since.

"After I graduated from YWAM, I worked in a street ministry in Hollywood. The third day out, a black girl punched me in the face three times. I didn't respond. I didn't even defend myself; I only felt compassion for her. The old Stacey would have taken her down. I realized then that I was free.

"I can't find any references to a spirit of anger in the Bible. Jesus didn't bind a spirit of violence when He delivered Legion, for instance. I do know that my childhood anger and bitterness somehow gave access to something that took control of me. I don't think I was totally demonized, but if it was just my lousy personality and my poor coping skills, how can someone cast that out in a moment? I know that when Tom prayed for me something shifted and I felt an instantaneous change that years of behaviour modification and communications courses did not address. This was something that I couldn't do by just wanting to be a better person, something that my attempts at good behaviour didn't fix. I still don't quite know how to process it. I just know that I'm free and I'm glad!

"I can't make a formula out of it and apply it to other people, or even apply it to other areas of my life. All I know is that I used to get in fights and I would not stop. I didn't care if I was going to get killed or not. I just wanted to make that person suffer and as soon as I drew blood I was satisfied. That's what I was like – and after that prayer, it was all gone – something was healed or cast out or delivered or whatever. I was free and have been since."

"I served with YWAM in the Philippines for six years, working in the Manila city garbage dump, home to 20,000 squatters. We did primary health care, evangelism and church planting. I returned to the States and completed my medical education as a physician's assistant at Stanford University in California. I then worked with the Peace Corps as a medical officer in Uzbekistan and Kiribati, a tiny island in the Central Pacific Ocean, for two terms of two years each. On summer holidays, I started going into Mozambique on evangelistic outreaches with teams from my church's school of ministry. Each time I would stay longer.

"I've been in and out of Mozambique for seven years now. I moved there three years ago. I can't say I live there full-time, because I spend about three months in Kiribati each year to earn wages to support myself in Mozambique. I work long enough to meet my expenses – which are quite minimal as I live in a tent."

Before I conducted this interview, I told Stacey that I was writing a new book and only briefly described its broad outline because I wanted to bias her as little as possible. Given some of the stories I'd heard from her fourteen years on the mission field, I simply said that I'd be very interested in her reflections on deliverance and spiritual warfare. This was her response:

"I became a Christian twenty-eight years ago and I've sought after authentic faith from the beginning. My pursuit has been to know Christ as He defines Himself, not as a culture defines Him or a denomination or a movement defines Him. When I first went overseas I was twenty-four and I realized when I was in a Filipino culture that a lot of my Christianity wasn't Christianity at all, it was just American.

"When I come back to the States to visit there is always a new Christian fad going around and there is no way I can keep up with it all. I hear things and see trends that I don't see a biblical precedent for. That is particularly the case when it comes to spiritual warfare.

"I live in what is considered by some to be one of the most demonic cultures in the world and I have certainly seen demonic manifestations. When I go into the bush the villages are typically under the authority of the local witch-doctor. When we are conducting our evangelistic outreaches, there are often people writhing about in the dirt. If we don't intervene, the local pastors start beating the person that's manifesting. They literally try to beat the demons out. We beg them: 'No, no, no – just leave them.' I've found that works best. I pretty much ignore the one manifesting. What I say is, 'Let's all just worship the Lord and put our attention on Him.' When we start worshipping, the demonized settle right down.

"Now I know people the world over are very hungry for attention and there are some who will do just about anything to get the spotlight, so I suspect a lot of what is going on is that wounded and lonely people are wanting attention.

"I do believe that there are people oppressed by demons – I've seen it. But I think we make *way* too much of an issue out of it. My approach is to downplay it; to be quiet. I'm not going to get in a screaming match with someone who is demonized.

I just quietly rebuke it and then turn the focus on Jesus and that usually takes care of it.

"Certainly beating the demonized person has not produced much fruit. All that happens is that they end up all bruised and terrorized and it draws a lot of attention away from Jesus. I haven't seen screaming and yelling work either, trying to cast out the spirit of this or of that. What I have been impressed with is 'hug deliverance'. There are times when we sit down in the dirt and we wrap our arms around the tormented and we love on them, all the while praying the blessing of God's presence. And as we worship, the torment dissipates.

"In one of our village outreaches, two blind witch-doctor women came to the meeting. Two children led them in. They were sitting in the front of the church where the older women usually sit, right up close. Their eyes were totally covered with cataracts. A Mozambican's irises are black as coal, but their eyes were cloudy white. We had a young nineteen-year-old guy from my home church preaching – the very first time he'd ever preached. He had been studying the local village beliefs; he would present a local belief and then he'd talk about Jesus. He spoke of the fear and anxiety and oppression that they lived with daily and then compared it with God's love, grace and mercy. He didn't explicitly address demonic issues or speak about healing.

"He gave a very simple invitation to those who wanted to respond to Jesus. The two witch-doctors were among the first to stand and as soon as they did they were instantly healed! They could see!

"There was no deliverance ministry. We didn't address demonic things or witchcraft at all. Nothing – just, 'Stand up if you want to make Jesus the Lord of your life. Stand if you want to repent of your sins and receive Jesus.'

"Of course the whole village knew these powerful women – so it was great. When word of their healings went round the village, everyone received the Lord.

"I once led an outreach in a very remote area. We came across a trail that went off the dirt road into the bush. It was large enough to suggest that there was a significant population, so I said, 'Let's see what's at the end of this trail.' We bounced along in our 4×4 truck and soon came to a village. A man came to greet us; it just so happened that he was the high priest for the Zionist church for that region. (I asked about the Zionists. Stacey said, "They're a very demonic bunch. They practise blood sacrifices and dedicate their children to the devil. They sing their worship songs to the pastor of the church, not to God.")

"We sat and talked with this pastor. He showed us a small pocket Portuguese Bible. He had underlined a good part of it and he seemed to be studying it carefully, so we talked to him at length and after about an hour I got to lead him to the Lord. It was Sunday morning; he said, 'My church is meeting here in about an hour. Would you stay and tell my church what you've told me?'

"I couldn't pass up an opportunity like that! I gave a really basic, Billy Graham-type Gospel message and the whole church ended up receiving the Lord, including a couple of witch-doctors. It was their suggestion to gather together their paraphernalia that they used for witchcraft and burn it. So the entire village all ran back to their huts and brought out their amulets, their sacred bone collections and things like their knives that they use for animal sacrifices. We had a roaring good bonfire and a huge celebration. But there were no demonic manifestations. No demonstrative events – no writhing in the dirt, hissing, or Darth Vader voices. Just lives set free.

"That pastor and his son have since gone through Iris' pastoral training programme and it is a strong, healthy Christian church now.

"It's not that I haven't seen some of the wild manifestations during deliverance, but I don't go looking for it. When it happens I address it. We try to minimize it because we know the devil is a showboat and he wants attention. But just as the Bible doesn't give much attention to the devil, we don't want to either.

"I had to deal with a demonized guy when I worked at the garbage dump in Maputo, the capital city of Mozambique. I was working with Iris, doing a clinic there. One day while I was preparing my medical kit, a man ten metres away from me was causing significant trouble. The local pastors were dealing with him as best as they could, but they weren't getting very far. He looked as though he was high on solvents.

"He was a big man and he was growling, threatening and posturing. I don't know how much was demonic, how much was his inebriation, and how much of it was him just wanting attention. I'm wondering about this while I'm messing with my kit – I'm down on my knees and suddenly I see this big black arm reach in to grab some of my drugs. I reflexively backhanded the thief in the face.

"Then I looked up and realized it was the guy who was manifesting. He was furious not only because I'd hurt him, but also because everyone had started laughing at him. He pulled back and was just about to plough me into the ground with his fist when I just reached up, put my hand on his heart and started praying. He had no idea what I was saying. He just sank down to his knees and started crying. I kept praying for him and he settled down, sobered up and later appointed himself as my bodyguard.

"I didn't cast any devils out of him. I just prayed in English and prayed in tongues, and got back to work."

"Village Mozambicans are spiritists and are heavily involved in witchcraft. They know the power of a curse and they live a lot of their lives in fear. But we can be fearful apart from the devil's involvement. I think a lot of it is right here, in our minds. This is where the battlefield is. If we slide into unbelief, doubt and anxiety, there is a natural fall-out. There is also an opportunity to let the devil get in there and wreak havoc.

"I had a patient in the States who was severely, chronically, clinically depressed – she had been institutionalized for years, on every medication imaginable. She was under psychiatric care; she'd had shock therapy – the whole gambit. She was a disaster.

"I went overseas for almost a decade and on my return a woman approached me one day and gave me a big hug. I didn't know who she was. I asked, 'Have we met?' She said, 'Yes, I'm Karen.'[3] I still didn't know who she was. Then she pulled out an old photo, taken during her days in the psychiatric ward. I was astounded – 'Karen!'

"She then began to tell me of an encounter with God that totally changed her life. Unbelievably, she'd been released from the hospital. She went home severely depressed and tried to commit suicide. She took all her pills, but someone came by to visit, found her unconscious and took her to the hospital. Her stomach was pumped and when she woke up in intensive care she was even more depressed because she couldn't even get killing herself right.

"Karen was desperate enough to call for a pastor. My pastor, Bill Johnson, was the one who came to visit. She was expecting sympathy and pity. He heard some of her story and then said, 'Karen, you need to repent. You've been giving yourself over to this depression. You need to fix your eyes on Jesus and choose life, not this mess you've gotten yourself into.' She was so furious she threw him out of the room.

"But then she thought about it and figured, 'I've tried everything else and nothing's worked.' So she decided to approach the depression as a sin issue rather than as the consequence of a hormonal or chemical imbalance, a dysfunctional upbringing,

---

[3] Her name has been changed.

or something else medical. She just said, 'God forgive me for getting into this depression.'

"Amazingly, she was set free. Not only was the depression gone, but she was filled with joy, to the extent that several months later her house burned down in a forest fire and she laughed all the way through it. It was as if nothing could get her down.

"When I was working in that town for a season, I would tell other depressed patients about Karen. I'd say, 'I'll pay for you to have lunch with her. If you're still depressed at the end of the hour, I'll give you all the medicine that you want.' They rarely came back to see me.

"In the charismatic world, we attribute so much to the devil. A lot of the time I think we try to absolve ourselves of personal responsibility when it comes to issues of depression or fear or anxiety. We can predispose ourselves to sickness and the demonic if we have opened our life, through wilful rebellion or long-term bitterness, and often if we just repent, that will take care of what we think is a demonic stronghold. Now, there probably is demonic influence at work. The devil gets in there and takes his opportunity when we give him a foothold. But I don't think we have to go through an exorcism, or the sprinkling of holy water or a song and dance. Just pray: 'God, forgive me . . .' and that restores the standard of wholeness.

"Without question, we live in a spiritual environment. I guess what I'm saying is that I think that the Christian streams I see in the West often overemphasize the dark side of it and give it more status and power and recognition than it deserves. I don't want to underplay the demonic and say these things don't exist – that it's all superstition. We're walking a tightrope.

"When we see patients at our clinic in Manica, we assess their presenting problems and then try to discern: is this illness demonic, is it hormonal, is it chemical, is it an infectious disease. We try to it approach it at every level. But we always pray for them first.

"Before we even open the clinic in the morning, we present the Gospel to the crowd that has gathered. Then we start seeing patients. The first room in our clinic is the prayer room. They have to get through there before they ever get to the medical treatment. Some things are just healed right there at the doorway. But if they don't get healed – and the vast majority don't – then I treat them medically.

"Having said that, we see a lot of healings – supernatural healings. I have seen broken bones mend. I have seen it right before my eyes. I love that. I think all disease is a result of sin and the fall. It's not a part of God's original design, it's not a part of God's Kingdom and there is no disease in Heaven. A person is created in God's image and disease in a person is trespassing. It has no right to be there. So I pray for them and if that doesn't work then I'll use my medical skills and resources and do whatever I can. I will use all my resources to try to deal with the illness. As a certified physician's assistant, I have seven years of formal scientific study behind me and I am pretty pragmatic. A 'supernatural realist'.

"Not all disease is necessarily spiritual. For example, if I have a poor diet and I don't get Vitamin C, I will get scurvy. I don't think a demon gave me scurvy – it was the consequence of my poor diet. How do you 'deliver' a person from starvation? You can't cast it out. What they need is nutritious food. Mission medicine requires continuous discernment. If you have conjunctivitis, a very common eye infection here in Mozambique, God can supernaturally cure it and sometimes He does. Other times antibiotics cure it – easily. It's a very real tension for us. I say, let's address disease on every level and cover all of the bases. Let's start with prayer though. But if a person is not healed supernaturally, I have some medical expertise and some medicine and I am going to use all of my resources at hand."

[Stacey laughed.] "There's still so much I don't understand. When we are preaching on our outreaches, we often have a reoccurring phenomenon that we don't know what to do with.

Witch-doctors regularly come and curse us and it often feels like a spear goes right thought your back. It's excruciating. Because it happens so often, we have a plan. If that happens to me and I'm incapacitated, I'll sit down and the next person gets up and keeps on preaching. The others on the team will pray for me and the pain disappears. We presume that God's blessing out-performs the witch-doctor's curses. We pray – it takes a few minutes – and then it goes away. But then the next preacher gets 'stabbed!' They sit down and while we're praying for them, someone else takes over the preaching.

"We don't quite understand why we don't have the Lord's full protection, or why we only experience these knifing pains in the Manica region. We haven't experienced it anywhere else. It's weird.

"I do know that it's witchcraft. We're camping in the jungle and we hear the witch-doctors beating their drums at night. We've got a drum and we beat 'em back. We worship and our rhythm is quite a bit better. And we bless them. We return blessings for the curses, but we still get 'stabbed' while preaching.

"There is a lot I honestly don't understand. We pray for sick people. Many don't get healed. Some do. If there is a formula, we haven't found it.

"I had a woman come to me at the Iris centre in Zimpeto. She was one of the cooks and six months before I saw her she had torn some ligaments in her knee. It was still swollen and she could hardly walk on it. After examining it I told her that there was absolutely nothing I could do. It needed surgery. I said, 'All I have to give you is prayer. We have nothing to lose.'

"Now, I had not a grain of faith in my heart that it would help. It was just, 'This is what I am supposed to do.' I had no faith for her healing. She had no faith either, but she said 'Okay, pray.' God healed her.

"We both started dancing around the clinic. She danced her

way out of the clinic. The next day she came back with a friend who had a messed-up knee. Now I'm full of faith, the two of them are full of faith, we pray for this third person and nothing happens.

"I have no faith in God and He heals the first woman and the next time I have all the faith in the world and nothing happens. No formula. Same prayers, same people, same place – one day apart. Honestly, there's lots I don't get.

"What I do understand is a warfare of love and kindness. It's kindness that draws people to repentance. It's not threats of hell and manipulation. It's God's tender mercy. The spiritual warfare that we're engaging in is simply focusing on Jesus and demonstrating His love. Like the Scriptures say, 'They will know we are Christians by our love, one for another' – not by our orphanages or our medical clinics or our Bible schools or our programmes. The Mozambicans watch us like hawks. They post people in trees to observe us, so we very loudly demonstrate love to one another, because we know they are watching and listening. And that has won more success than all of our prayer vigils and prayer meetings and our attempts at trying to break this or that stronghold."

Chapter 9

Armour for What Fight?

"Forgiveness is an aspect of power, establishing a moral supremacy which reminds everyone that the balance of power has shifted."
(Nelson Mandela)[1]

One of the moments that precipitated the writing of this book took place in casual conversation. I no longer remember the context, but a friend said, "I put on my armour every single day before I get out of bed." In response, I asked a simple question: "Do you take it off every night?" He looked at me and then we laughed, because no, he didn't. We then joked about layer after layer of armour accumulating, wondering if, like a child over-bundled in a snowsuit, that might explain some of the Church's present ineffectiveness.

My friend was certainly not alone in his daily ritual. A sense of spiritual vulnerability causes many to move towards all manner of superstitious acts. As a young teenager, I never went anywhere without my lucky rabbit's foot. As long it was in my pocket, I was sure that all would be well. This is in no way to equate the armour of God with a lucky talisman. But we are called to be men and women of faith, not magic. What I suggested to my friend was that instead of his normal routine, he give *thanks* for the Lord's graced protection every day.

✣ ✣ ✣

1 Anthony Simpson, *Mandela*, HarperCollins, London, 1999, p. 523.

The famous Ephesians 6:10 passage begins with the word *"Finally"*. Other than the final greetings, Paul's spiritual armour teaching is the conclusion to all that he has written in his letter. This conclusion, however, reads retrospectively, for in the apostle's mind his understanding of spiritual conflict is set in an explicit context, one that he named at the opening of the letter. It is a context of grace: *"Blessed be the God and Father of our Lord Jesus Christ, who has conferred on us every spiritual blessing in the heavenly realms."* [2] God's desire to bless is greater and more far-reaching than any power to curse. It has been since before the foundation of the earth – and before the cosmic rebellion – and will be for whatever time remains. [3]

Further, we would also do well to re-read the apostle's prayer in Ephesians 3:14–21 before considering our engagement with the powers, for the reminder of our true identity and our position in Christ is the ground on which we *"stand firm against the stratagems of the devil"*. [4] Among other things, Paul prays that *"with deep roots and firm foundations* [we may] *be strong to grasp what is the breadth and length and height and depth of Christ's love, and to know it, though it is beyond knowledge"*. [5] We engage the enemy knowing that, as Paul declared in Romans, *"nothing . . . can separate us from the love of God in Christ Jesus our Lord."* [6]

Paul's first admonition is that we *"find* [our] *strength in the Lord, in his mighty power"*. [7] The verb tense is passive imperative, meaning this is something to which we must attend, but in the knowledge that the strength of which Paul speaks is an external infusion of power, not a stirring of our own internal resources. This is the fulfilment of his opening prayers, that we might

---

[2] Ephesians 1:3.
[3] Markus Barth, *Ephesians*, Anchor Bible Commentary, vol. 34A, Doubleday, Garden City, NY, 1974, p. 760.
[4] Ephesians 6:11.
[5] Ephesians 3:16–18.
[6] Romans 8:39.
[7] Ephesians 6:10.

know *"how vast are the resources of* [God's] *power open to us who have faith"*.[8] It is also what he prayed in his apostolic prayer, that *"out of the treasures of his glory, he may grant* [us] *inward strength and power through his Spirit"*.[9] We engage the inferior powers as heirs of the incomparable power that was demonstrated in the resurrection of Christ. The war has already been fought and won. Christ is now seated in the heavenly realms, *"far above all government and authority, all power and dominion, and any title of sovereignty that commands allegiance, not only in this age, but also in the age to come"*.[10]

It is for this reason that Paul calls believers to a defensive posture. Ephesians 6:10–17 is not a call to arms for the purposes of defeating the enemy. That has already been accomplished, so the outcome is never in doubt. God does not need further recruits to turn the tide of the conflict. We are simply admonished to *"stand firm against the stratagems of the devil"*.[11] We are not called to fight our adversary; we merely face his *stratagems*. Chrysostom comments, "[The devil] does not overcome by force, nor by tyranny, nor through compulsion, nor through violence. [Otherwise] he would have destroyed all men."[12] He continues: "This enemy is at war with us, not simply, not openly, but by 'wiles.'" These Chrysostom defines as deception, artifice, contrivance and seduction, and concludes that the devil does not "gain anything by the conquest, but that he may despoil us".[13] It is for this reason also that Paul says that we only *struggle* against demonic forces. The Greek word is not one taken from a military context or the battlefield, but rather comes from the

8 Ephesians 1:19.
9 Ephesians 3:16.
10 Ephesians 1:20–21.
11 Ephesians 6:11.
12 *Against Those Who Say that Demons Govern Human Affairs*, Nicene and Ante-Nicene Fathers, First Series, vol. 9, Hendrickson Pub., Peabody, Mass., 1994, p. 187.
13 Homilies on Ephesians, XXII, Nicene and Post-Nicene Fathers, First Series, vol. 13, Hendrickson Pub., Peabody, Mass., pp. 159–160.

world of sport, specifically the gymnasium and is therefore sometimes translated as "wrestle".[14]

Chrysostom gives our struggle extended consideration in a sermon titled, *None Can Harm the Man Who Does Not Injure Himself.* He surveys the demonic assaults that came against the Bible heroes Job, Joseph and Paul. He says of the apostle, "Did he not experience innumerable storms of trial? And in what respect was he injured by them? Was he not crowned with victory all the more in consequence?" Chrysostom concludes:

> "In no case will anyone be able to injure a man who does not choose to injure himself, even if all the world were to kindle a fierce war against him. For it is not stress of circumstances, nor insults of men in power, nor intrigues besetting you like snow storms, nor a crowd of calamities, nor a promiscuous collection of all the ills to which mankind is subject, which can disturb even slightly the man who is brave and temperate, and watchful."[15]

Though it is only a wrestling match, we do have a considerable adversary. Paul states: *"Our struggle is not against human foes, but against cosmic powers, against the authorities and potentates of this dark age, against the superhuman forces of evil in the heavenly realms."*[16] This comprehensive list points far beyond individual human sinfulness and wickedness. With even the briefest review of the last century, it is the only way to understand the horrors of human history, for the evils perpetrated have been so obscenely greater than the sum of the atrocities committed by wicked men.

In 1944, Raphael Lemkin created the word "genocide". It was required to define the unbelievable crimes against

---

[14] KJV and NKJV.

[15] Chrysostom, Nicene and Post-Nicene Fathers, First Series, vol. 9, Hendrickson Pub., Peabody, Mass., p. 279.

[16] Ephesians 6:12.

humanity of World War II. The word is a hybrid from the Greek *geno*, race, and the Latin *caedere*, killing. Genocide is not war, it is "race murder". It is the slaughter of women, unarmed children and non-military men. Genocide is the "intentional annihilation and eradication of a whole culture".

In 1915, the Ottomans slaughtered over a million Armenians with the hopes of "purging the nation". Under the Nazis' Final Solution, over six million Jews and "undesirables" were exterminated. Stalin killed more Ukrainians than Hitler did Jews and condemned over eighteen million "dissidents" to slave labour in the gulags. The "lowest credible" number of deaths under Stalin is a conservative twenty million, but some estimate it to be as high as fifty million casualties. During Mao's twenty-six year regime, it is estimated that at least forty million Chinese were put to death. Another thirty million perished in the famine during the disastrous three-year Great Leap Forward. From 1975–1979, Pol Pot's four-year reign of terror in Cambodia left two and a half million dead – in a country of seven million. Bosnian Serbs eradicated two hundred thousand non-Serbs in 1992–1995. During that same period, Rwandan Hutus systematically butchered the Tutsi minority, slaughtering eight hundred thousand in one hundred days; over a million perished before killing stopped – one of every eight in the nation.[17]

Death by atrocity has taken unnumbered millions in a long list of countries that include: Ethiopia, Nigeria, Bangladesh, Mozambique, Afghanistan, Congo, Yugoslavia, Myanmar, Tibet, Algeria, Sudan, Vietnam, Angola, East Timor, Iraq, Uganda, Kurdistan and Somalia.

Many more millions die because of the West's lifestyle of privilege. In a most provocative book, *The Corporation: the Pathological Pursuit of Profit and Power*, Joel Bakan documents the gross social irresponsibility of many multinational companies. One example follows:

[17] Samantha Power, *A Problem from Hell: America and the Age of Genocide*, Basic Books, NY, 2002.

Eighty percent of the world's population that lives in developing countries represents only twenty percent of the global market for drugs. (The entire African continent represents only 1.3 percent of the world market.) Conversely, the twenty percent of the world's population who live in North America, Europe and Japan constitute eighty percent of the drug market. Predictably, of the 1400 new drugs developed between 1975 and 1999, only 13 were designed to treat or prevent tropical diseases and 3 to treat tuberculosis. In the year 2000, no drugs were developed to treat tuberculosis, compared to the 8 for impotence or erectile dysfunction and 7 for baldness. Developing drugs to deal with personality disorders in family pets seems to have a higher priority than controlling diseases that kill millions of human beings each year."[18]

In his novel, *The Grapes of Wrath*, John Steinbeck gave eloquent voice to the superhuman forces that destroy human life. During the Dirty Thirties, destitute sharecroppers in Oklahoma were forced off their land. Steinbeck says of the corporate "owner men":

"All of them were caught in something larger than themselves. Some of them hated the mathematics that drove them and some were afraid, and some worshipped the mathematics because it provided a refuge from thought and from feeling . . . . The Bank – or the Company – needs – wants – insists – must have – as though the Bank or the Company were a monster . . . [that] breathes profits. If they don't get it, they die the way you die without air . . . . The Bank – the monster has to have profits all the time. It can't wait. When the monster stops growing, it dies. It can't stay one size . . . . The Bank is something more

---

[18] Joel Bakan, *The Corporation: the Pathological Pursuit of Profit and Power*, Penguin, Toronto, 2004, p. 49.

than men. It's the monster. Men made it, but they can't control it."[19]

Walter Wink has done a commendable job in his considerations of social justice, economic and political structures, and the *"authorities and potentates of this dark age"*. Those interested in exploring these issues are referred to his two books, *Engaging the Powers* and *Unmasking the Powers*.

Incredibly, against the overtly demonic forces yet at work against us, what the apostle Paul would have us do is *"take up the armour of God . . . and stand* [our] *ground"*.[20] Four times in the space of four verses, Paul admonishes us to *"stand"*. He may well have had in mind the counsel Moses gave to the Israelites. They had just been delivered from captivity in Egypt and oppressive life under one of the more demonic cultures in human history. Pharaoh and his armies were nearly upon them and the people of Israel were not only terrified; blame, resignation and hopelessness were rife. In the midst of all of the complaints, Moses answers, *"Have no fear; stand firm and see the deliverance that the LORD will bring you this day . . . The LORD will fight for you; say no more."*[21]

It has been said that *"the gospel of peace* in context of military metaphor is a lofty paradox"*,[22] yet it is the very thing that *"[gives us] firm footing"*[23] and enables us to stand. Paul does describe a very unusual armour – the gospel of peace, the belt of truth, a breastplate of integrity, a shield of faith, the helmet of salvation and the Word of God – against the cosmic

---

[19] John Steinbeck, *The Grapes of Wrath*, Bantam, NY, 1946, pp. 32–35; cited in *Engaging the Powers*, Walter Wink, Fortress Press, Minneapolis, 1992, p. 50.

[20] Ephesians 6:13.

[21] Exodus 14:13–14.

[22] Markus Barth, *Ephesians*, Anchor Bible Commentary, vol. 34A, Doubleday, Garden City, NY, 1974, p. 770.

[23] Ephesians 6:15.

powers of evil. But the nature of the conflict is such that when
we are at peace with God we make war with the devil.[24]

In this, we do not stand alone. The entire armour passage is
addressed not to an individual believer, but to the Church. The
pronouns are all plural. In Texas they would say, correctly,
"Y'all stand together..." The whole metaphor is a corporate
calling. This especially casts the taking up of the *"great shield of
faith"* in new light. The shield Paul names is not the small,
round, garbage can lid of a shield, but literally the *thyreos*,
derived from the word *thyra*, meaning "door".[25] A Roman
soldier would hold this shield in his left hand and the right two-
thirds of the shield would cover his left side. The left third of the
shield covered his mate's exposed right. When the troops were
in position, they created a defensive formation called the
"tortoise". When the legionaries held their shields overhead
and the front rows interlocked their shields, they created a kind
of shell-like armour that shielded them against missiles both
from above and out front.[26]

In these tight ranks, each soldier was dependent on the other
for protection. One suddenly understands why there have been
so many casualties in church, for we have characteristically
been far too individualistic in our understanding of warfare. It is
not hard for many of us to think of those who are no longer in
ministry, or even church. They fought a valiant fight, but
because no one was standing at their side, they were vulnerable
targets for the *"burning arrows of the evil one"*[27]

The last piece of armour that Paul names is *"the sword which
the Spirit gives you, the word of God".*[28] It is the very weapon that

---

[24] Chrysostom spoke this truth the other way round. Homily XXIV, Nicene and
Post-Nicene Fathers, First Series, vol. 13, Hendrickson Pub., Peabody, Mass., 1994,
p. 167.

[25] Ephesians 6:16; Markus Barth, *Ephesians*, Anchor Bible Commentary, vol. 34A,
Doubleday, Garden City, NY, 1974, p. 771.

[26] Kate Gilliver and Michael Whitley, *Rome at War*, Osprey Pub., Oxford, 2005,
p. 113.

[27] Ephesians 6:16.

Jesus used victoriously against Satan's temptations in the wilderness.[29] As has been demonstrated a number of times throughout this book, the conflict with the devil is won or lost in the realm of truth, not power.

In this regard, it is germane to consider a verse from Matthew's Gospel, for it is one that regularly features in the contemporary conduct of deliverance ministry. Jesus says to Peter, *"I will give you the keys of the kingdom of heaven; whatever you bind on earth will be bound in heaven, and whatever you loose on earth will be loosed in heaven."*[30] The Lord then speaks explicitly of His imminent suffering, death and resurrection. With Peter's newly commissioned authority to bind and loose still ringing in his ears, the impetuous disciple thinks he'll have a go. Peter tries to "bind" such a horrible outcome for his beloved Lord. Literally, Peter *rebukes* Jesus. (This is not Peter's brightest moment.) This *rebuke* is the same word that is used repeatedly in the context of demonic deliverance: Jesus rebukes the demonized man who interrupts in the synagogue;[31] He rebukes the demonized epileptic;[32] and He rebukes the violent storm at sea.[33]

As to Peter's actual attempt at the binding, the NIV translates the Greek idiom as *"Never, Lord"*, but the phrase is stronger than that. It is an invocation for the overturning of evil and should be rendered "God forbid", or, as the REB does, *"Heaven forbid!"* However it is translated, it doesn't go well for Peter. Jesus doesn't applaud Peter's first attempt, encouraging him with a "Nice try, Peter." Rather, Jesus reprimands him: *"Out of My sight, Satan .... You think as men think, not as God thinks."*[34]

---

28 Ephesians 6:17.
29 Matthew 4:4, 7, 10.
30 Matthew 16:19, NIV.
31 Mark 1:25.
32 Matthew 17:18.
33 Matthew 8:26.
34 Matthew 16:23.

Such a stern response implies that Peter seriously mis-understood and misused the binding and loosing authority that had been entrusted to him. Peter was not the only one to do so, for there are some who use these verses to legitimize a ministry focused on binding the strongman and his demonic horde.

Jesus bound the strong man and despoiled his goods.[35] The Greek word is the same as in the binding commission given to Peter. But the disciples are never given the authority to bind the strongman, nor is there ever any reference to the need to do so on an ongoing basis. Jesus did it, past tense. The disciples are repeatedly authorized to heal and cast out demons, but they are never instructed to bind them. Scripture does contain clear and unambiguous binding and loosing mandates that *are* delegated however: we are to *"bind up the broken-hearted"*,[36] and *"loose the chains of injustice"*.[37]

There is one deliverance account where both binding and loosing are used together, and it is the only other time that binding is used in connection with deliverance.[38] Satan had kept the crippled woman bound for eighteen years; Jesus loosed her one Sabbath.[39] In delivering the woman, Jesus did not have to bind the devil. That He had already done; He was now despoiling his goods. It is worth noting that this is the only occasion in the Gospels that loosing is used in connection with deliverance. Characteristically, demons are *"cast out"*.[40]

The particulars of the binding and loosing commission given to the disciples are given a clear context in Matthew 18:18. The exact same wording is used as in 16:19: *"whatever*

[35] Matthew 12:29.
[36] Isaiah 61:1.
[37] Isaiah 58:6, NIV.
[38] Luke 13:10–16. The local villagers had unsuccessfully attempted to bind Legion with chains. Mark 5:3–4.
[39] Luke 13:16.
[40] Matthew 8:16, 31; 9:33; 10:1, 8; 12:27–28 etc.

*you bind on earth will be bound in heaven, and whatever you loose
on earth will be loosed in heaven."* The instruction that precedes
the repeated commission has to do with relational dealings
with those who sin against us. That is followed by further
instruction on unlimited forgiveness. Jesus then tells the
parable of the unmerciful servant, which concludes with
the corporate admonition to *"forgive your brother from your
hearts".*[41]

All of these verses have to do with interpersonal reconcili-
ation. Our willingness to forgive and be forgiven – or our
unwillingness – determines not only our present relational
health and wellbeing, but has eternal consequence. This is
what we bind and loose. There is no biblical basis for the
binding of evil spirits, or the "breaking off" of spirits of
depression or alcoholism or anything else in order to "loose"
someone.

I have mentioned Nev Green earlier in this book. He has
become one of my closest friends. He is one of my most regular
ministry hosts and over the last six years he has travelled with
me on about a third of my annual trips. We've come to
thoroughly enjoy one another. The Lord has also partnered us
together in very special ways, for his giftings and mine have
grown to complement one another. I'm a better preacher when
he leads worship and he says that the worship he gets to lead is
qualitatively different when I'm the one preaching. Our hosts
concur.

It has never happened to date, but were Nev and I to have a
falling out, such that neither of us wanted to travel with the
other, it would have ministry consequences beyond the rift in
our friendship. If I were to "bind" my grievance against Nev
here on earth, it would "bind" Heaven's fruitfulness because
we were no longer working in blessed partnership. Conversely,
if we were to "loose" forgiveness to one another, that would

---

[41] Matthew 18:35.

"loose" a further release of Heaven's blessings as we continued to serve together.

Nev and I have intentionally established a foundational commitment to one another. We've each said to the other, "I love you too much to allow you to offend me."

Most study Bibles list John 20:22–23 as a cross-reference for the binding and loosing verses. There the resurrected Jesus says, *"Receive the Holy Spirit! If you forgive anyone's sins, they are forgiven; if you pronounce them unforgiven, unforgiven they remain."* Forgiveness in any form, let alone unconditional, unlimited forgiveness, is certainly not a natural inclination. Rather, it is a supernatural grace, the work of the Spirit of God in and through us. And a declaration of forgiveness is always a deathblow to the work of the enemy. As a proclamation of truth, it wins the fight against the deceptions and the lies that the evil one perpetrates. By refusing to be offended, we re-establish Kingdom rule and authority, heart by heart, and we thereby tyrannize the powers of darkness.

The armour of God is given to us for defensive protection, not aggression. For instance, Paul does not name the Roman soldier's seven-foot spear as part of the *panoplia* – the soldier's full and complete armour. In this spiritual conflict, the saints do not respond to evil in kind.

I was working on this very chapter during Holy Week and things suddenly became very clear. Jesus rode into Jerusalem *"on a donkey, on the foal of a beast of burden"*.[42] Matthew says that the prophecy in Zechariah 9:9 had been fulfilled: *"Here is your king, who comes to you in gentleness."* The full quotation reads: *"See, your king is coming to you, his cause won, his victory gained, humble and mounted on a donkey, on a colt, the foal of a donkey."* Though victorious, Jesus does not come as a king of war,

---

[42] Matthew 21:5.

mounted on a stallion. Rather, He "[disarms] *the cosmic powers and authorities ... leading them as captives in his triumphal procession"*[43] by the power of gentleness and humility.

In Ephesians 6:13, Paul says that as we stand our ground in the conflict, we literally "finish the job".[44] The word *katergazomai* elsewhere in Paul's writings typically means "to accomplish, to complete, or to bring about". Just as Jesus won victory over the powers in gentleness and humility, so we overcome the same way.

Jesus was horrendously victimized the last few days of His life. He was betrayed, abused, tortured and finally exterminated. Though victimized, Jesus was never a victim. His life was not taken from Him; He gave it freely. The powers of darkness were unable to make Jesus be whom they wanted Him to be; they could not kill the life that was in Him. A victim's overwhelming and incapacitating sense of powerlessness is what empowers an evil perpetrator. Through His victorious death and resurrection, Jesus rendered the powers impotent, so thoroughly defeating the last enemy, death.

It is in this very reality that we are called to *"stand"*. Victims do not, cannot *"stand"*. Only victors can. And just as Jesus spoke forgiveness from the cross, in the midst of the very worst of His victimization, forgiveness is the power that transforms victims into victors.

Few of us have not been victimized in some manner or other. Some have had to endure all manner of horrible, wicked and abusive treatment. A victim's identity ultimately involves the abdication of personal responsibility: "I am what I am because of what was done to me." It is true that it is not for us to take responsibility for what happens *to* us. We are responsible for what happens *within* us. If we adopt a victim's identity,

---

43 Colossians 2:15.
44 Markus Barth, *Ephesians*, Anchor Bible Commentary, vol. 34A, Doubleday, Garden City, NY, 1974, p. 765.

we become accomplices to the powers that victimize and "finish their job" for them.

The foundation of the Gospel is the very core of a transformed personhood: that in spite of what anyone else might think, in spite of whatever other treatment I might receive, God counts me as His beloved child, unique, prized and unconditionally loved.

The power of forgiveness, gentleness and humility are the "weapons" that we use *"against cosmic powers, against the authorities and potentates of this dark age, against the superhuman forces of evil in the heavenly realms"*. Victims do not have the resources to forgive. Only victors do. Only in Christ, with our focus on Him, are we empowered to stand in our true identity in Him. Because we know ourselves to be forgiven we are empowered to "finish the job" and overcome all that comes against us, from any source, knowing that there is *"nothing . . . that can separate us from the love of God in Christ Jesus our Lord"*.[45]

Only victors can "turn the other cheek".[46] Victims cower and take yet another beating. Jesus said, *"If anyone slaps you on the right cheek, turn and offer him the other also."* Why the right cheek? The explanation is best understood interactively.

A *punch* with the right fist lands on the *left* cheek of the one struck. So does a right-handed slap.

A blow to the right cheek would require using the left hand, but in a right-handed world, the left hand was used only for unclean tasks. To strike someone on the right cheek with the right hand can only be done with the back of the hand.

The violence perpetrated here is not the first blow of a potential fistfight, but that of insult. A backhanded slap conveys contempt. It is not an attempt to incapacitate. The purpose is not so much to injure the body, but to wound the spirit. A backhand slap was the cultural norm for admonishing inferiors:

---

45 Romans 8:38.
46 Matthew 5:39. I am indebted to Wink's insights, *Engaging the Powers*, Fortress Press, Minneapolis, 1992, pp. 175–77.

masters backhanded slaves; husbands backhanded their wives; parents backhanded their children; Romans backhanded the Jews.

In the Sermon on the Mount, Jesus was speaking to the *am hararitz*, the people of the land, the poor and the poor in spirit. When He says, *"If anyone slaps you . . . wants to sue you . . . forces you to go one mile. . . "* He was speaking to people who knew all too well what it was to be the subjects of these very indignities, the victims of class, age, gender, status and race.

Why, then, the counsel to turn the other cheek? Such an act of radical humility robs the oppressor of the power to humiliate. The aggressor cannot backhand the left cheek – at least with the same hand he first used. In a world that ruthlessly observed the rules and regulations governing what was clean and unclean, the left hand would not be used and to strike with a fist would make the other an equal – a peer, not a subordinate.

In offering the left cheek, there is a moment of transformation, from victim to victor. And as Martin Luther King and Nelson Mandela demonstrated, that inner personal transformation ultimately disarms the distortions and deceptions of the *"powers and principalities"* that fuel prejudice, hatred and fear, for "no lie can live forever".[47]

---

[47] *The Autobiography of Martin Luther King Jr.*, ed. Claybourne Carson, Time Warner, NY, 2001, p. 33.

Chapter 10

Contrary Engagement

"These devils keep us in terror,
because we lay ourselves open to being terrorized."

(Teresa of Avila)[1]

✣ ✣ ✣

I have eight round beach stones on one of my study bookshelves. They are precariously balanced on top of each other. It took a great deal of patience, trial and error to find the equilibrium that weighed out all the differences. Once I got them into perfect position, they've maintained that static balance now for years.

My life in Christ is rarely so static. Things just don't seem to stay put for very long and I'm learning to live with the dynamic tensions of all that is constantly changing. As difficult as it is, I've come to conclude that those very tensions, more than balance, are the essence of faith. A vital relationship can never be static.

If one could ask the apostle Paul the simple question, "Are you saved?" his answer would not be a simple, static and balanced one. He might well have grinned and said, "That depends. Do you mean, *so-theis, sodz-o-me-nos,* or *so-thei-sei?* If *so-theis,* gloriously so; if *sodz-o-men-os,* more than yesterday, less than tomorrow; if *sodz-o-men-os,* not yet."

---

[1] *The Life of Teresa of Avila,* trans. J. Cohen, Penguin Books, Edinburgh, 1957, p. 182.

So-theis is an aorist passive participle. It marks a single, completed act in the past, one which has present, even eternal consequences. Paul uses this verb tense when he declares that *"[God] desires all men to be saved and to come to the knowledge of the truth."*[2] One would use this verb tense when answering the question, "When were you saved?" It marks the beginning of our new life in Christ.

But that conversion moment is the start of a present and ongoing process. Paul uses the present participle, *sodz-o-men-os,* conveying this truth thusly: *"The message of the cross is foolishness to those who are perishing, but to us who are being saved it is the power of God."*[3]

And while we are being saved, there is also a future dynamic to faith. *So-thei-sei* is a future passive verb and points to our glorious resurrection, the final consummation, and the fulfilment of all of the "not yet-ness" hopes of our faith. *"If, when we were God's enemies, we were reconciled to him through the death of his Son, how much more, now that we have been reconciled, shall we be saved by his life!"*[4]

Salvation is so comprehensive it is at the same time a past fact, a present experience, and a future hope. The apostle Paul would have us understand that we have been saved, forgiven and cleansed by Jesus' shed blood. We are being saved through the process of our ongoing sanctification, as the Spirit continuously transforms our lives; and we will be saved and know in fullness the eternal destiny that yet awaits us at the consummation. Every day, we live out the dynamic tensions of the past, present and future consequences of our salvation in Christ.

We need this same sense of dynamic tension in our understanding of deliverance and warfare. Paul writes, *"[God] enthroned Christ] at his right hand in the heavenly realms, far*

[2] 1 Timothy 2:4, NKJV.
[3] 1 Corinthians 1:18, NIV.
[4] Romans 5:10.

above all government and authority, all power and dominion, and any title of sovereignty that commands allegiance, not only in this age, but also in the age to come. He put all things in subjection beneath his feet, and gave him as head over all things." [5] This passage marks a single, fully completed act in the past, but one which has present, even eternal consequences.

Though we have been *"rescued [past tense] from the domain of darkness and brought into the kingdom of his dear Son"*, we still *"wrestle [present tense] . . . against powers . . . [and the] rulers of the darkness of this world".* [6] While we are already victors in Christ, we continue to struggle against the stratagems of the evil one.

And while we stand our ground, we yet await the final consummation, for *"in putting everything under him, God left nothing that is not subject to him. Yet at present we do not see everything subject to Him."* [7] We live in hope, knowing that *"the end will come, when he hands over the kingdom to God the Father after he has destroyed all dominion, authority and power. For He must reign until he has put all his enemies under his feet."* [8]

It is this dynamic tension, even more than balance, which we live on a daily basis.

The apostle John says, *"you are strong; God's word remains in you, and you have conquered the evil one."* [9] Literally, John says we have the physical strength to overcome, because the Word of God abides in us and in that overcoming, we *"have conquered"* our enemy. The apostle uses the perfect verb tense to convey the fact that in our abiding we appropriate both the victory that Christ has won over the evil one and the delegated authority that Jesus gave His disciples. That authority is succinctly declared in Luke 10:19, *"I have given you the power to tread*

---

[5] Colossians 1:13; Ephesians 1:20–22.

[6] Ephesians 6:12, KJV.

[7] Hebrews 2:8, NIV.

[8] 1 Corinthians 15:24–25, NIV.

[9] 1 John 2:14.

underfoot snakes and scorpions and all the forces of the enemy.
Nothing will ever harm you."[10]

Even though we have a defeated enemy over whom we have
authority, we continue to contend for all that is ours in Christ.
Writing during a period of intense persecution, the apostle
Peter warns, *"Be on the alert! Wake up! Your enemy the devil, like a*
roaring lion, prowls around looking for someone to devour. Stand up
to him, firm in your faith, and remember that your fellow-Christians
in this world are going through the same kinds of suffering."[11] The
verbs used are either present participles or infinitives, implying
that the devil is continuously attempting to instil fear, ever
looking for opportunities to consume and is insatiable in his
desire to devour.

In this, one also has to decide what Jesus meant when He
promised, *"Nothing will ever harm you."* Certainly the early
Church believed that it was more than life in an insulated little
bubble. Tradition holds that all but the apostle John were killed
for their faith.[12] How could so few, in such a short time, so
radically transform one of the greatest empires of human
history?

The Lord's protection enabled those first disciples to lay
down their lives in the knowledge that death would not
harm them. Tertullian was one of the first of the church
fathers to write on martyrdom and he did so graphically.
Addressing the heathen rulers he taunts: "Go on – rack,
torture, grind us to powder: our numbers increase in propor-
tion as you mow us down. The blood of Christians is their
harvest seed."[13]

Similarly, Chrysostom used one of the Kingdom parables to
explain the supernatural growth of the Church in the face of

[10] Luke 10:19.
[11] 1 Peter 5:8–9.
[12] *Fox's Book of Martyrs*, ed. Wm. Forbush, Winston, Chicago, 1926, pp. 2–5.
[13] Philip Schaff, *The History of the Christian Church*, vol. II, Grand Rapids,
Eerdmans, 1883, p. 76.

Rome's ruthless and bloody persecution: "The power of the righteous has its force not in the magnitude of their number, but in the grace of the Spirit. There were twelve apostles. Do you see how little is the leaven? The whole world was in unbelief. Do you see how great is the lump? But those twelve turned the whole world to themselves." [14]

If all of this is not unsettling enough, there is a single verse of Scripture that generates greater dynamic tension than all the rest combined. It is found at the end of the Lord's model Kingdom prayer: *"Do not put us to the test, but save us from the evil one."* [15]

At face value, the confusions raised at the thought of a gracious God leading His beloved children into temptation are extremely perplexing.

As is always the case, context is everything. Temptation and deliverance must be understood in light of the coming of the Father's Kingdom, here on earth. How many in Heaven are tempted to steal? How much adultery is going on in Heaven? How often do the angels have to break up the fights? What prejudices divide and what injustices oppress?

We are to pray, "As in Heaven, so here on earth." [16] Heaven is the perfect fulfilment of God's will and is now our model. In Christ we've changed the way we think about life. Sin has lost not only its hold, but also its draw. We're in love with true love and all lesser loves have lost their appeal.

Nevertheless, there is wisdom in recognizing a measure of exposure. We are still "in the flesh" and while no one in Heaven needs deliverance, the evil one is at work against us here on earth. An example serves. Under the sovereign providence of God, the apostle Paul was *"buffeted by a messenger of Satan"* [17] The Greek word translated as "buffeted" literally

---

[14] Chrysostom, p. 192.
[15] Matthew 6:13.
[16] Matthew 6:10.
[17] 2 Corinthians 12:7.

means "fist"; here its verb form means "to strike violently with the fist". It is also in the present, active form, implying ongoing abuse, and as such, graphically describes the pounding that Paul was taking.

In the midst of the attack, the Lord answered Paul's heartcry for deliverance by establishing more of the Kingdom's reign and rule in Paul's spirit. The apostle does not say whether the problem was solved, or if the buffeting came to an end. His focus was so thoroughly shifted, for he had appropriated ongoing victory in the Lord's revelation, *"My grace is all you need; power is most fully seen in weakness."*[18]

While meditating on those words, my morning Bible reading happened to be the story of the stilling of the storm.[19] A *mega-seismos* – literally "a great shaking" – suddenly arose. As the phrase is typically used in connection with earthquakes, it's a most unusual word to describe a storm at sea.

The disciples, most of whom were professional fisherman, were terrified. Presumably they were afraid of drowning – afraid of death – even though they were in the immediate presence of the Lord of Life. In contrast, Jesus remained in perfect peace, heedless of the intensity of the storm. He was abiding in that which *"cannot be shaken"*.[20]

All manner of things begin to break open at this point. So much of popular writing on spiritual warfare puts the focus on the circumstances that come against us – the buffeting, the storms and the great shakings – without seeing behind or beyond to the context of the attack.

The panicked disciples woke Jesus from His deep sleep. Graciously, He rebuked nature gone berserk and then asked the disciples, *"Where is your faith?"* As I was thinking about

[18] 2 Corinthians 12:9.
[19] Matthew 8:23–7.
[20] Hebrews 12:27.

all that was being shaken in my own life, it seemed that the Spirit was asking me a further question: "In what is your faith?"

I have it settled that my faith is never in my faith, as in, "Do I have enough faith to rebuke all that is raging against me?" Rather, my faith is ever in His faithfulness – and in that, I believe that the present storm I'm living in, whatever its nature, in no way disconcerts Jesus. It then seemed that I was asked, "Do you believe that the offer of *'peace . . . which is beyond all understanding'*[21] extends to even this shaking?"

Standing in that peace is my victory.

As we exercise faith in the loving faithfulness of God, we cut off the enemy's "supply lines". As we deepen our relationship with our Heavenly Father, His graced covering calms our fears and anxieties, and we know something further of the battle strategy of Psalm 46, that in the midst of war, and the shaking of all that can be shaken, we can enter His rest, knowing that His sovereign authority extends to all that conspires to come against us. We are invited to a confident stillness in the knowledge that it is He who actively engages the enemy: *"He puts an end to war: he breaks the bow, he snaps the spear, he burns the shields in the fire."*[22] It is for us to join the victory chorus and declare, *"The* LORD *of Hosts is with us; The God of Jacob is our fortress."*[23]

In trying to make all of this *schtem*, Chrysostom used a phrase that I found very suggestive. He said that the demons "were eating the devil's garbage".[24] I find it a very insightful picture that helps me understand deliverance ministry. Demons are like

[21]　Philippians 4:7.

[22]　Psalm 46:8–9.

[23]　Psalm 46:9–11.

[24]　Nicene and Ante-Nicene Fathers, First Series, vol. 9, Hendrickson Pub., Peabody, Mass., 1994, p. 191.

rats. When we turn on the light, they scurry for the cover of darkness. They haven't disappeared; they're still lurking about in whatever darkness they can find. We don't need to trap them or call in an exterminator. What we need to do is put out the garbage they feed on.

Origen brought forth further insights in his work, *On the Opposing Powers*. He spoke of the "the seeds of sin" and commented,

> "When we have indulged [our appetites] beyond what is proper, and have not resisted the first movements to intemperance, then the hostile power, seizing the occasion of this first transgression, incites and presses us hard in every way, seeking to extend our sins over a wider field . . . and, if possible, beyond all limits." [25]

If we are computer savvy, we know that we are literally a keystroke away from demonic influence. A simple pop-up during an internet search could initiate what Origen calls "the first movements to intemperance". And with all of the rubbish that's on TV these days, a careless click of the remote control could amount to the "first transgression" that serves a feast of garbage that the rats are craving.

It can happen so innocently. Several years ago, a friend and I went to an out-of-town pastors' conference and on our return to the hotel room, my friend was channel surfing in search of the evening's basketball game. The TV carried some porn programmes and for just a moment, my friend lingered on the naked body that was suddenly displayed. I was quick to say, "Turn the channel. Life is a series of choices. We can't go there."

Mixing metaphors, these are just a few of the ways we "put the trash out" and in so doing, "cut off the enemy's supplies".

---

[25] Ante-Nicene Fathers, vol. 4, Hendrickson Pub., Peabody, Mass., p. 330.

The teachings of the Church's spiritual masters have been a considerable resource in understanding both dynamics.

Antony of Padua lived over sixteen hundred years ago. He was a great man of prayer and served the sick and the demonized with notable spiritual authority. He also offered tested counsel:

> "When [the demons] come, their actions correspond to the condition in which they find us; they pattern their phantasms after our thoughts. Should they find us frightened and distressed, immediately they attack like robbers, having found the place unprotected. Whatever we are turning over in our minds, this – and more – is what they do. For if they see that we are fearful and terrified, they increase even more what is dreadful in the apparitions and threats and the suffering soul is punished with these. However, should they discover us rejoicing in the Lord, thinking about the good things to come, contemplating things that have to do with the Lord, reflecting that all things are in the hand of the Lord and that a demon has no strength against a Christian, nor has he any authority over anyone – then seeing the soul safeguarded by such thoughts, they are put to shame and turn away." [26]

And though he wrote nearly twelve hundred years after Antony, the Spanish master, Ignatius Loyola made a similar point:

> "The enemy's behaviour is like that of a military leader who wishes to conquer and plunder the object of his desires. Just as the commander of an army pitches his camp, studies the strength and defences of a fortress, and then attacks it on its weakest side, in like manner, the

---

[26] Athanasius, *Life of Antony*, trans. Robert Gregg, Paulist Press, NY, 1980, p. 63.

enemy of our human nature studies from all sides our theological, cardinal and moral virtues. Wherever he finds us weakest and most in need regarding our eternal salvation, he attacks and tries to take us by storm."[27]

Chrysostom's instruction is also a great help in understanding how it is the demonic tries to effect our ruin.

"An eye was given, in order that we may behold the creation and glorify the Master. But if we do not use our eyes well, they become to us the ministers of adultery. A tongue has been given, in order that we may speak well, in order that we may praise our Creator. But if we are careless, it becomes a cause of blasphemy. And hands were given that we may stretch them forth in prayer. But if we are not careful, we stretch them forth unto covetousness."[28]

I have been aware of the power of careless words for some time now. To consider what comes out of our mouths as blasphemous puts things in a new light, for I previously only thought of blasphemy in terms of taking the Lord's name in vain. But any time we give the devil and his works more attention than they deserve, any time we speak in judgement against one another, or find fault with God's governance of our lives, we are ultimately speaking against the name of God and all that He is. That "trash talk" not only gives the demonic garbage to feed on, it also supplies the enemy with all manner of resources to come against us. Jesus repeatedly spoke against careless words: *"Listen and understand! No one is defiled by what goes into his mouth; only by what comes out of it."*[29] *"Plain 'Yes'*

[27] Ignatius of Loyola, *Spiritual Exercises*, trans. Anthony Mottola, Image Books, 1964, p. 132.

[28] Nicene and Post-Nicene Fathers, First Series, vol. 9, Hendrickson Pub., Peabody, Mass., p. 188.

[29] Matthew 15:10–11.

or 'No' is all you need to say; anything beyond that comes from the evil one.''[30]

All of these insights serve as commentary on Jude 6, where we read that the fallen angels are *"bound in darkness, with everlasting chains"*. One aspect of the tension in which we live is that the demonic, while bound, nevertheless have a limited sphere of influence.

In this, I think back to my days as a paper boy. One of the houses on my route had a huge, snarling German Shepherd that guarded the front yard. The dog terrified me, until I realized that he was on a heavy length of chain. At the extremity of his lead, he had worn a clearly marked path and as long as I was on the far side, I had nothing to worry about. His heavy chain was my protection.

As long as we stay out of the demonic realm, we have no worries. Should we enter their territory, we put ourselves at risk. This is exactly the counsel the great reformer John Calvin offered:

> "Satan has many wiles and he attacks us by many strange tricks, but God gives us sufficient armour, as long as we ourselves do not want to be deceived. We have therefore no reason to complain that the darkness is stronger than the light or that truth is conquered by falsehood, but rather when we are led astray from the right way of salvation, we are paying the penalty of our own carelessness and indolence."[31]

Putting out the garbage and cutting off the enemy's supplies are two of the ways we contend for our freedom and our peace. Ignatius of Loyola names yet another strategy that is ours in this fight. He says, "It is the nature of our enemy to become

---

[30] Matthew 5:37.

[31] John Calvin, *Commentary on 1 Timothy 4.1; A Calvin Reader*, ed. William Keesecker, Westminster Press, Philadelphia, 1985, p. 110.

powerless, lose courage and take to flight as soon as a person who is following the spiritual life stands courageously against his temptations and does exactly the opposite to what he [the devil] suggests."[32] The phrase "a warfare of opposites" is pregnant with insight. It succinctly summarizes the very posture we are to take as we stand. The evil one comes against us with lies and deceptions. Armed with *"the sword which the Spirit gives us, the word of God"*[33] we defend ourselves with truth and revelation. We conquer torment with peace. And when all manner of disasters befall us, we turn our complaints into praise.

This warfare of opposites has even broader application, for consideration needs to be given to an approach to ministry that tries to attend to the devil's "legal right to torment". Because of past sins and ungodly involvements, there are some who encourage that we need to work through a "spiritual inventory" with the view to "closing off the access points". But that's the wrong strategy. It is a "works" righteousness, even if we're working to appropriate all that is ours in Christ. This in no way diminishes the need to repent and be forgiven. But anything more has us trapped in quicksand. When, or how, can we ever get to the bottom of our unrighteousness?

At conversion, when we come to Christ and ask forgiveness for our sins, we do not confess them one by one. Many of us would have explicitly confessed the grievous sins that weighed heavily upon us at that moment. That is only right and appropriate. We are not, however, required or able to conduct a ruthless inventory and confess every sin we ever committed. As the psalmist wrote, *"Who is aware of his unwitting sins?"* With him, we pray, *"Cleanse me of any secret fault."*[34]

Do the demons have a legal right to torment me? Yes, because I am not yet sanctified. I will not argue with their claimed rights,

[32] Ignatius of Loyola, *Spiritual Exercises*, trans. Anthony Mottola, Image Books, 1964, p. 131.
[33] Ephesians 6:17.
[34] Psalm 19:12.

but neither will I fight them on their terms. Rather, I wage a warfare of opposites and use the ultimate weapon against their inferior tactics. I do not dispute my unrighteousness; mine, however is the Gospel declaration, *"Mercy triumphs over judgement."*[35] I boldly stand in the grace that is mine in Christ, and remind myself, *"There is now* NO CONDEMNATION *for those who are united with Christ Jesus. In Christ Jesus the life-giving law of the Spirit has set* [me] *free from the law of sin and death."*[36]

The alternative goes something like this. I diligently work through the spiritual inventory and close all the ungodly access points I can. I feel great – for two weeks – until – I start wondering if I might have missed something. And then, I'm sure I missed something, for the accuser has started up with his torment again.

There will always be more condemning accusation to come, whether in the form of the "sins of the fathers", or my own, previously forgotten failings. Judgement is pending. But mercy always triumphs. It's not a fair fight.

Any time we try to sort our lives, by any means, we are seeking to self-justify. We are fighting on our enemy's battlefield, attempting to fight with his weapons. We not only come under the accuser's ongoing torment, we will ultimately lose that war.

By way of contrast, there are graced moments when the Holy Spirit brings to light something of our past. There is never any condemnation in that merciful revelation. It is always revelation unto further wholeness and holiness. We must, however, be able to discern the difference between the conviction that the Revealer stirs, and the condemnation that the accuser imposes. Conviction is always that which empowers confession, redemption and sanctification. Condemnation breeds self-loathing, fear and further oppression.

---

[35] James 2:13.
[36] Romans 8:1–2, emphasis added.

Over four hundred years ago, Teresa of Avila offered wise and warning counsel:

> "These devils keep us in terror, because we lay ourselves open to being terrorized .... By loving and desiring what we should loathe we have become our own enemies .... We make them fight against us with our own weapons, which we put into their hands instead of using them in our own defence." [37]

[37] *Teresa of Avila*, trans. J. Cohen, Penguin Books, Edinburgh, 1957, p. 182.

Chapter 11
Intimacy and Authority

"Why do you marvel [at these deliverances]*?*
It is not we who do it, but Christ, who does these
things through those who believe in Him.
What we have is not skill with words,
but faith through love that works for Christ."
(St. Antony of Padua, 4th century)[1]

The city of Ephesus was not only an important seaport; it was also the capital of the region and the gateway to Asia. The birth of the church in Ephesus represents a strategic moment in the mission of the early Church, for the seven churches named in Revelation 1:11 were all planted under Paul's influence from Ephesus: Smyrna, Pergamum, Thyatira, Sardis, Philadelphia and Laodicea, plus two more – Colossae and Hierapolis.

It was in Ephesus that Paul was used of the Lord to work *"extraordinary miracles"*. The sick were cured of their diseases and the demonized were delivered.[2] The next verse implies that these wonders inspired seven itinerant Jewish exorcists, for they *"tried their hand at using the name of the Lord Jesus"*.[3] They were seduced by the apostle's success and attempted to apply whatever formula they had deduced by observation. However,

---

[1] Athanasius, *The Life of Antony*, The Classics of Western Spirituality, Paulist Press, NY, 1980, p. 89.

[2] Acts 19:11–12.

[3] Acts 19:13.

they had neither a personal relationship with Jesus, nor any Kingdom authority.

In the midst of their attempts at delivering a demonized man, the evil spirit responded, *"Jesus I recognise, Paul I know, but who are you?"* [4] (That may be the single most humiliating question in all of Scripture.) What follows was not at all pretty. *"The man with the evil spirit flew at them, overpowered them all, and handled them with such violence that they ran out of the house battered and naked."* Luke employs considerable understatement when he says that *"everybody in Ephesus ... got to know of it".* [5] A single demonized man chasing seven naked and terrified "wannabe" exorcists through the city does necessarily draw significant attention!

By way of contrast, the Church saw marked success as it grew quickly, even amongst those practicing sorcery, for *"the word of the Lord showed its power, spreading more and more widely and effectively"* [6]

As Luke tells these two stories back to back, he uses the same word in Greek, *isquoe*, "to be strong", and demonstrates that while the demonic can overpower, the Word of God is the greater power.

One of my ministry hosts, Dr. Dave Mullen, relayed his favourite deliverance that more than illustrates this truth. At the end of the third service of the weekend, Dave felt exhausted. He had spent himself preaching and ministering.

"Before I could slip out the door and head for home, someone tapped me on the shoulder and said, 'Pastor, I think you need to pray for that lady at the altar.' A tiny woman – under five feet tall – was receiving prayer from several members of our prayer ministry team. I walked forward and stood quietly next to this woman seeking to discern the Lord's heart for her. After a few moments, I gently touched her

[4] Acts 19:15.
[5] Acts 19:16–17.
[6] Acts 19:20.

shoulder and asked her if there was anything specific she'd like me to pray for.

"With that her head snapped toward me and with bared teeth and a guttural snarl she said in a deep voice, 'I just want to kill you.' That was not the sort of answer I had been expecting.

"More out of exhaustion than faith I burst out laughing and said, 'No, not today and not here.' She started to manifest visible anger and was physically and vocally very agitated. It seemed that her demon wanted to be taken seriously. But instead of generating fear, the wilder things got, the funnier it seemed to me. I just laughed harder.

"Finally, with a simple command that it be gone, it was over. It was the easiest deliverance time I have ever been through. A short time of prayer and counsel followed and we all went home, finally.

"More than a year later this little lady is still with us and is well on the road to wholeness. She has been receiving ongoing counselling to deal with some significant experiences of abuse from her adolescence. I believe these unresolved issues provided the ground for the demonic to gain its footing."

As easy as Dave's "laughter deliverance" was, there is a marked contrast in the unsettling story of the demonized boy with epilepsy. While Jesus, Peter, James and John were descending from the Mount of Transfiguration, the remaining disciples tried, unsuccessfully, to cast the evil spirit out. The gathered crowd had become cynical and the disciples were frustrated. When Jesus arrived, the boy's father brought a telling indictment to bear: *"I asked your disciples to drive it out, but they could not."*[7] Jesus quickly and easily delivers the boy from a deaf and dumb spirit and restores the child to health.

Privately, the disciples ask afterward, *"Why could we not drive it out?"* Jesus answers, *"This kind cannot be driven out except by*

7   Mark 9:18.

prayer and fasting."[8] It is safe to assume that the boy was not plagued with a demon of stubbornness.

Prior to the deliverance, Jesus did not call a series of prayer meetings and assign a five-day fast. Rather, He delivered the boy there and then. In the deliverance He demonstrated effortless power. Yet He says, *"This kind cannot be driven out except by prayer and fasting."*

I misunderstood these words for most of my Christian life. As a young teenage believer, I was mentored by the Navigators. I am forever indebted for the years of disciplined Bible study and memorization. Much of my zeal was fuelled by one of their oft-repeated sayings: "If your intake isn't greater than your output, your upkeep will be your downfall." That doggerel served well as motivation for my quiet times in the early years. But it also fed an unhealthy performance orientation.

Previously, I understood the Lord's words about prayer and fasting in terms of achievement. If I could put in enough hours on my knees and missed enough meals, somehow, somewhere, the cosmic balance would tip from curse to blessing, and I could then make something happen. No matter how hard I tried, however, I always seemed to fall short.

I now understand prayer and fasting differently. The input isn't unto output – in this case, the deliverance. In John 15:5, Jesus says, *"Apart from me you can do nothing."* I am taking that word more seriously than ever, and in its light, I understand that prayer and fasting are not unto achievement, but rather are yet another call to abiding in Christ.

A conversation with my friend Bruce broke this open for me. Two years ago he ran the Boston marathon. I used to run in my mid-twenties and always dreamed of running a marathon. There was a piece of me (certainly not my knees) that was envious of Bruce's ability to qualify for the prestigious Boston.

8 Matthew 17:21; Mark 9:29.

As I asked about his preparations, he told me that he'd been training diligently for *three years*, slowly building up from his regular weekly run of forty miles. Along the way, he'd entered and qualified in several marathons before the Boston. All of that rigorous training and deposit in his runner's bank account allowed him to make a very large withdrawal come the big day in Bean Town. He had the authority to run in one of the world's greatest races only because he had spent so much time abiding, mile after mile, for several years of training. What motivated all of these long, arduous runs was simple: Bruce loves running.

When my friend worked me through all of those details, I suddenly thought of George Müller of Bristol, who, in the late 1800s, lived a life of uncommon faith and regularly saw miracles in his midst. George habitually spent four hours a day in prayer. I couldn't understand how that was possible until I read his biography.

Near the end of his life, he affirmed that for seventy-three years he had read and re-read the Bible over two hundred times.[9] I did the math. On average, that meant that he read through the entire Bible every four and a half months. My Bible contains just over a thousand pages and on that basis, George would have read roughly seven pages of Scripture per day. He said that half of his Bible reading he did "on his knees". That meant he read *very* slowly – four pages in four hours. Further into his biography, I learned why it took him so long.

Müller said he had two aspirations: "To get my heart into such a state that it no longer has a will of its own," and "To look to the Word, inspired by the Holy Spirit, to know His heart and purposes." As to the length of time he spent in prayer, George said, "Would the believer therefore have his faith strengthened, he must *give God time to work.*"[10]

---

[9] Basil Miller, *George Müller: Man of Faith and Miracles*, Bethany House, Minneapolis, 1941, p. 22.

[10] *Ibid.*, p. 59, italics in text.

Knowing the heart and timely purposes of God are the essence of spiritual authority. Intentions like Müller's are the only way I know to shift from the self-centred prayer attitude that essentially says, *"My* will be done ... in Jesus' name,"* to a Spirit-controlled abandon that cries, "Holy is *Your* name ... Your Kingdom come...."

Many of us have learned that there are no short cuts in this maturing process. Extended time alone in the secret place cannot be compromised for we have come to know most intimately the truth of Hebrews 4:12:

> *"The word of God is alive and active. It cuts more keenly than any two-edged sword, piercing so deeply that it divides soul and spirit; it discriminates the purposes and thoughts of the heart."*

The more we put our hearts and our hearts' affections before the Word of God, the more He transforms our lives, conforming them to the image and authority of Christ.

I still have a long way to go. Jesus answered John the Baptist's question, *"Are you the one who is to come?"* saying, *"Go and report to John what you hear and see: the blind recover their sight, the lame walk, lepers are made clean, the deaf hear, the dead are raised to life, the poor are brought good news."*[11] Earlier, Jesus had commissioned His disciples with the very same mandate: *"Go, preach this message: 'The kingdom of heaven is near.' Heal the sick, raise the dead, cleanse those who have leprosy, drive out demons."*[12] It is of particular note that the cleansing of lepers was not an expectation of messianic authority. It is not in the prophetic mandate of Isaiah 61 for instance.

Rather, it is a distinctive of the ministry of Jesus. When a leper approaches Him and pleads, *" 'If you are willing, you can make me clean,' Jesus reached out his hand and touched the man. 'I am willing,' he said."*[13] Unlike those around Him, Jesus had

[11] Matthew 11:3–4.
[12] Matthew 10:7–8, NIV.

absolutely no fear of the leper's contamination or defilement. The healing demonstrates that the power of wholeness and holiness is always the greater and that there is no life so foul that Jesus can't make it pure.

Lamentably, it is possible to love praying for the sick more than one loves the sick. It is also possible to love casting out demons more than one loves the demonized. But one cannot cleanse a leper in a power encounter. Something in the touch, the gentle, physical contact itself heals – if not the diseased skin, then certainly the "dis-eased" heart.

The apostolic commission to *"heal the sick, raise the dead, cleanse those who have leprosy,* [and] *drive out demons"* is an extension of Jesus' ministry. The power and authority that is to be exercised in His name is not raw power, but the power of love and the authority of compassion.

It is profoundly sobering to realize that when we find ourselves in situations where we ask the disciples' question, *"Why could we not drive it out?"* the answer may be that it's not so much that we don't have enough power to drive out demons; it's that there's not enough love.

---

[13] Matthew 8:2–3.

Chapter 12
Battle Plans

"The supreme art of war is to subdue the enemy without fighting.
Thus, what is of supreme importance in war is
to attack the enemy's strategy."
(Sun Tzu, *The Art of War*)[1]

✢ ✢ ✢

While interviewing my friend Dr. John, I asked lots of questions, for he has worked with some profoundly tormented "individuals". The last word is in quotes because several of his patients were diagnosed with Dissociative Identity Disorder and presented many different "individualities", each with their own name, voice and personality. None of them could be considered healthy; rather, they were very evidently demonized as they were ruled by fear, lies, deceptions and gross distortions of reality.

In the course of our conversations, Dr. John mentioned that while the different presenting personalities knew that there were others in company with them, they knew nothing of any of the other's identity. With a flash of insight, I suddenly knew why. Community is a gift of God for the people of God. The demonic, by nature, knows nothing of true communion. Having forfeited the right to life and love, theirs is an isolated existence.

One of the enemy's strategies is to impose that same sense of isolation on his victims. In all manner of ways he seeks to

---

[1] *The Art of War*, trans. Samuel Griffith, Oxford, 1963, p. 77.

estrange us from one another, perpetually attempting to sow discord and division.

The power of a loving community demonstrates the very opposite dynamic. I asked Elliott Tepper, the founder and director of Betel International, to reflect on the changes he's seen over the course of Betel's history. One of the questions I asked was, "Why did you deliver so many men from demons in the early years, yet dramatic deliverance ministry seems to happen very rarely now?"

Elliott answered, "When we first started out, we used to get some really demonized men. They were wild, rebellious, almost unmanageable. Looking back, it was like it was a power struggle, a test to see if we would stay the course. We were on the bottom of the learning curve.

"It seems that over two decades we've demonstrated that Jesus is indeed our victory.

"On our outreaches, we still see deeply demonized types of people wandering the streets, but they are no longer willing to come into our centres. It's like they know that there's no contest. The light that shines in us is too bright.

"The demons haven't gotten 'weaker' *per se*; we've gotten stronger. I think we have a lot more authority than we used to have. More and more people are coming to Christ, lives are being transformed, more and more churches being planted and we're taking significant ground.

"When a heroin addict comes into one of our centres, there is a good chance that he's under some demonic influence. His life has certainly been hell. And just by joining us as we worship, as we turn our hearts towards God, his life, like a dirty cup, is stuck under the tap. It gets cleaned out as fresh water flows through it. The more water that flows through it, the cleaner it gets.

"Hearing the Word of God, studying it, taking part in the devotionals, working together, living together; those are all sanctifying influences.

"Twenty years ago, our community was small and very young. Now, Betel has grown and we have a much larger church body. The worship is vibrant, the preaching is strong, the communities are by and large healthy and so demons don't like to come near us.

"The devil doesn't want to be around light. We now have a lot of people full of God, we have a rich expression of the Body of Christ and that's not the kind of company the devil wants to keep."

The following story traces the ongoing deliverance and redemption of a man who was more intimate with the darkness than anyone I've ever met. His alias name is Sean Davies. We've become very special friends. He and I preached together at one of the sessions at the Detling Bible week in August 2004 and I look forward to every chance we have to be together. In August 2005, he and his wife were sent out as the senior leaders of one of the newest Betel communities in the UK.

I met Sean at Betel's founding centre in Madrid, October 1999. I interviewed him at length a month later for my book, *We Dance Because We Cannot Fly.*[2] It documents the glorious redemption of lives destroyed by heroin addiction. His story is detailed in Chapter 4, "Accelerated Grace". I interviewed him again four years later in October 2003, and asked specific questions about his understanding and experience of deliverance.[3]

Sean had a very strange upbringing. His father was a burglar. Drugs, crime, violence and abuse were "normal". He doesn't remember any overt occult influence that influenced his family.

He had a hard time growing up. Sean summarized his school years with this story: when a teacher hassled him for his

[2] Sovereign World, Tonbridge, 2002.
[3] Some phrases and brief sentences are taken from *We Dance Because We Cannot Fly.*

behaviour, he responded, "I'm not any good at being good; I'm very good at being bad."

Sean started using drugs when he was eleven years old. They were easily accessible – joints were kept in the fruit bowl on the kitchen table. In his early teens he was using heroin, cocaine and crack, and within a few years he was dealing, burgling and living the life of a gangster. By the time Sean was thirty-one he had a criminal record of thirty-eight charges. Many were for armed robbery; twenty-five were for burglary. Sean was in prison eleven and a half years. His last sentence – seven years – was served as a subversive prisoner in the infamous Dartmoor prison.

Sean confessed, "If Jesus hadn't gloriously delivered me from the absolute bottom, I'd either be dead or be doing life for killing a number of people. I certainly had plans."

I asked, "How did it get so bad, so desperate?" As perverted as it sounds, Sean conceded, "A personal relationship with the devil." Before burgling, he would pray, "If you help me get in and out with the goods, if you keep the police at bay, I'll serve you forever." When bullied, he repeatedly asked the devil to give him strength. "If you help me beat up these guys, I'm yours."

Sean has Chinese writing tattooed on his chest. The characters mean "Black Heart". The tattoo was an intentional choice because Sean wanted to be totally fearless. Given his criminal involvements, he couldn't afford to have any hesitations. However, it was not just a symbol, but a dark sacrament, sealed with a covenant. Sean was led to pray, "Satan, if you're there, if you are who you claim to be, do it. Make my heart black."

Sean said, "With that, I gave myself unconditionally to the devil. I felt his pleasure and I felt that my prayers had been answered. Thereafter, I never had any fear, and I wasn't a good fighter. I just figured that if I could get in one punch, it was worth a beating."

I asked, "How have you been brought back from the depths of the darkness?"

Without hesitation or deliberation Sean answered, "The love of Christ. The acceptance of being loved and the ability of being able to give love has saved me. The first evening I arrived at Betel, even though I was high, I could feel the love in the place. I could see it in everybody's eyes. And everybody was so kind to me. It was the first time that people have loved me for who I am, not for what I have to give them, or for what I could get for them. I wanted the kind of love I saw them demonstrating to me and to each other." He elaborated: "The enemy couldn't give me anything else. I'd had it all; done it all. It was all rubbish and I was sick of it. I didn't want to die anymore and I didn't want to be afraid of dying anymore."

Fed up, Sean completely surrendered – as much as he knew how – to Jesus and His way. "I'd gone the devil's way for thirty-one years – now it was the Lord's turn. I wanted to feel love . . . joy . . . to smile . . . to go to bed at night in peace. I felt an overwhelming zeal for life that said, 'Do not give up!' That was Jesus. That was the hand of God upon me, even though I didn't know Him. It was Him saying, 'Sean, keep fighting, keep pushing through. I will deliver you, because I am who I say I am and I will be your strength.'

"Jesus gave me the sense that He could put me back together. I felt that kind of release."

That was the first night of Sean's conversion. After fourteen days and nights of the worst cold turkey drug withdrawal he'd ever endured (Sean said he had pain in places that he didn't even know existed) he slept the deepest sleep of his life.

Sean was gloriously saved in November 1998, but as with all of us, his deliverence continues to be an ongoing process. Three years after his conversion Sean took part in a "Cleansing Stream" ministry course. Concurrently, he suddenly began to suffer stabbing chest pains. At first, no one linked the pain to the tattoo on his chest. Then during one session the Holy Spirit said to him, "Sean – remember all that the Chinese mafia prayed over you while you had that 'Black Heart' tattoo done. It was all said explicitly, for a purpose." After so many years of listening to the voice of the accuser, Sean was learning to listen to the Revealer.

It was still very much a process though, for one of biggest holds the enemy had on Sean was fear – especially the fear of being rejected. "It took a big step for me to open my mouth and talk about the tattoo. I didn't have to. No one knew the details."

A sense of shame was also being stirred. Part of Sean felt like this was something he should have dealt with a long time ago. "That's how twisted the devil can make things. But *this* was the time the Holy Spirit was saying, 'Let's get this sorted Sean.' It really is a process. You can't springboard and say 'I'll deal with this one first...' It's as the Spirit brings things forward."

I asked for clarification. For years, while shaving, Sean would be oblivious to the Black Heart tattoo, though he was staring at it in the mirror – just as he was oblivious to the scars on his body. With reflection, he could tell stories about each one – the beatings and the fights – but most of time he didn't even think about them. They were just there. It seemed that they'd been there forever and they'd be there forever.

With the Spirit's clear revelation, however, the Betel leaders and the others in the course prayed for Sean's deliverance. They also prayed for the divine exchange. Sean asked, "Lord, make my heart soft and full of love. Take the blackness out of it and let it be filled with light." The deliverance was evidenced not by the escape of screaming demons, but by complete and immediate freedom from pain and an overwhelming sense of God's love and His pleasure.

As part of that same interview I asked Sean, "As you read through the Gospels, do the deliverance stories in particular have any great significance?"

"I know exactly what's going on, especially with one – the story of Legion. Me and Legion were best friends for thirty-one years. I didn't run around in graveyards, naked and screaming, but I did run around the streets, absolutely crazy, life completely out of control.

"The devil controlled my actions and he controlled my emotions, and he controlled the direction and the path my life was taking at that time, but he didn't possess *me*, no, not at all. He just kind of rented vacant space. My heart was a 'loner' that was taken back.

"The Good News story that speaks to me most is John 5, the story of the cripple that can't get healed until Jesus comes by and asks, '*Do you want to get well?*'[4] For me, deliverance has never been a wrestle. Just a beautiful invitation. When I responded, Jesus booted Legion out of me without anything of a scuffle. He just strong-armed him right out of me. 'No rent paid,' so he was sent packing. Evicted."

"I don't feel ashamed about telling anybody about who set me free. I know where I've come from and I know what God's brought me out of. I've never been as happy in my whole life. Sometimes I might not seem happy, but on those days, you know, I was a lot worse out there. It's hard to explain; it's like I've got a big sun inside me, glowing. Where else could I find this freedom in life? I didn't find it anywhere else. Only in Jesus."

Our eyes are fixed on Jesus. Only on Jesus. As we struggle against the cosmic powers, we do so without looking at the enemy, for this is unlike any earthly fight.

I realize that previously I had been seduced by the deceiver. I'd been trying to fight the devil on his terms, on his grounds,

---

[4] John 5:6, NIV.

and respond to his tactics in kind, by and large in my own spiritual strength and without much authority. If honest, I have to confess that much of what I did in terms of warfare was motivated by fear and a sense of spiritual vulnerability.

But just as He does in every other aspect of life, Jesus has shown us another way. We wage peace through pre-emptive worship. We counter-attack with militant grace. We defend ourselves with aggressive gratitude. And we fight open hostilities with retaliatory humility, in the knowledge that *"there is nothing in life or death, in the realm of spirits or superhuman powers, in the world as it is or the world as it shall be, in the forces of the universe, in heights or depths – nothing in all creation that can separate us from the love of God in Christ Jesus our Lord".*[5]

Of this I am convinced.

Ad Majorem Gloriam Dei.[6]

---

[5]   Romans 8:38–39.
[6]   "To the greater glory of God."

Appendix A
Deliverance Prayers

"Jesus, we rest in the fullness of Your precious name, 'Saviour' (Matthew 1:21). Draw our hearts ever deeper in Your love and be our Way, our Truth and our very Life (2 Thessalonians 3:5; John 14:6). Thank You that You hold all things together – *our* all (Colossians 1:17). You are the Christ, 'The Anointed One'. We ask that You come to us and bring release to that which is still captive, and sight to all that is still blind. Bind up what's broken and grant us Your favour" (Luke 4:18).

"Holy Spirit, confer on us ever-more wisdom and understanding, that the eyes of our hearts may be enlightened, that we may know the hope to which You call us, how rich and glorious is our inheritance, and how vast the resources of power open to us who have faith (Ephesians 1:17–19). Reveal to us more of the Kingdom righteousness, peace and joy that is purposed for us (Romans 14:17). Lord, our hearts cry out – 'Your Kingdom come' – in us, through us and by us" (Matthew 6:10).

"Thank You Jesus that You have rescued us from the domain of darkness and brought us into Your Kingdom. Thank You that our release is secured and our sins are forgiven (Colossians 1:13–14). You are the light of the world and You give the light of life (John 8:12). Everything exposed to light becomes light (Ephesians 5:13); send forth Your light and Your truth to be our guide; draw us into Your dwelling place – there we lay everything before You, for You and You alone are our joy and delight" (Psalm 43:3–4; John 14:1–6).

"Father, we humble ourselves before You that we might know more of Your grace (1 Peter 5:5) and we pray that out of the treasures of Your glory, You would grant us strength and power in our innermost being, that Christ may dwell in our hearts in love. Lord, let it yet be ever-more established deep within us – the length and breadth, the height and depth of Your love for us in Christ; may we know it, knowing that this love is ever-beyond our understanding. Lord, fill us with this knowledge, that we would be filled with Your very fullness. Father, may we live with the expectation that You are ever doing immeasurably more than all we can ask or even conceive, all to Your glory, now and forever more" (Ephesians 3:14–21).

"Thank You, Father, that You purpose to conform us to the very image of the Lord Jesus; renew our minds, that our whole nature be thus transformed (Romans 8:29; 12:1–2). Holy Spirit – fill us with peace and joy, until we overflow with hope (Romans 15:13) and make us whole and holy, through and through, spirit, soul and body, free of any fault" (1 Thessalonians 5:23).

Appendix B

What's in a Name?

1. Jesus = Saviour (Matthew 1:21)

2. Friend of sinners (Matthew 11:19)

3. Light of the world (John 8:1; 9:5)

4. Victorious Lamb (Revelation 12:11)

5. Worthy (Revelation 4:11)

6. Giver of life (John 1:4; 11:25; 14:6)

7. The Truth (John 14:6)

8. Giver of every perfect gift (James 1:17)

9. Revealer (John 1:18)

10. King of kings (Revelation 17:14)

11. Above all government, power (Ephesians 1:21)

12. Destroyer of the destroyer (1 John 3:8)

1. Satan, Hebrew = devil, Greek = accuser, slanderer (Job 1–2; Zechariah 3:1; Revelation 12:10)

2. adversary, enemy (1 Peter 5:8)

3. Lucifer, bright morning star (Isaiah 14:12)

4. defeated dragon (Revelation 12:7)

5. Belial, worthless one (2 Corinthians 6:15)

6. murderer (John 8:44)

7. father of lies (John 8:44)

8. thief (John 10:10)

9. deceiver (Revelation 12:9)

10. prince of this world (John 12:31)

11. prince of power of the air (Ephesians 2:2)

12. destroyer (Revelation 9:11)

13. Deliverer (Matthew 6:13)

13. tempter (Matthew 4:3)

14. Heavenly Father (Luke 11:13)

14. evil one (Matthew 6:3; 13:38)

15. Alpha and Omega, the Beginning and the End (Revelation 1:8)

15. god of this passing age (2 Corinthians 4:4)

16. God of the living (Matthew 22:32)

16. Beelzebub, dung god (Mark 3:22)

17. Christ, Anointed One (Luke 4:18)

17. antichrist (1 John 4:1–4 = un-anointed one)

About the Author

Dr. Guy Chevreau served the Baptist church from 1979 to 1994. He received his Th.D. from Toronto School of Theology, having studied in the area of historical theology. Through his international teaching ministry begun in 1994, he has served interdenominationally in more than thirty-two different countries, ministering the Father's love, Christ's empowering grace, life in the Spirit, prayer and intercession, evangelism and compassion for the poor.

Guy is the author of *Catch the Fire*, the first published work to put the "Toronto Blessing" in some theological and historical context. Since its release in October 1994, *Catch the Fire* has been translated into twelve foreign languages. He is also the author of four other books: *Pray with Fire*, *Share the Fire*, *We Dance Because We Cannot Fly* and *Turnings*.

Guy is married to Janis and they have two children, Graham and Caitlin.

We hope you enjoyed reading this New Wine book.
For details of other New Wine books
and a range of 2,000 titles from other
Word and Spirit publishers visit our website:
www.newwineministries.co.uk